Sunset
Low-Fat
COOK BOOK

By the Editors of Sunset Books and Sunset Magazine

Sunset Publishing Corporation
Menlo Park, California

Research & Text
Cynthia Scheer

Special Consultant
Patricia Kearney, R. D.,
Clinical Dietitian,
Stanford University Hospital,
Stanford, California

Coordinating Editors
Deborah Thomas Kramer
Joan Beth Erickson

Design & Illustration
Sandra Popovich

Photography
Glenn Christiansen: 11, 46, 94;
Peter Christiansen: 3; **Kevin Sanchez:** 6, 14, 19, 22, 27, 30, 35, 38, 43, 51, 54, 59, 62, 67, 70, 75, 78, 83, 86, 91.

Photo Styling
Susan Massey-Weil

Healthy. . . and Simply Delicious!

Say "lowfat foods" to today's health-conscious cooks, and you'll conjure up images of dew-sprinkled fruits and crisp vegetables, gleaming fish, and market-fresh poultry. In this new lowfat cook book, you'll find recipes for preparing these and other light and luscious foods in a wealth of appealing ways. And if you think that lowfat cooking isn't satisfying—get ready for a surprise! Our book is full of recipes for dishes so robust and rich-tasting, they'll appease even the heartiest appetites. You'll discover chunky Harvest Turkey Soup, savory Oven Beef & Mushroom Stew in Bourbon, and hearty Green & Red Lasagne. You'll be able to satisfy your sweet tooth, too. From Peach & Raspberry Crisp to Liqueur Pound Cake, our desserts—like all our recipes—deliver delicious flavor with little or no fat.

All our recipes have been developed to conform to the American Heart Association (AHA) requirements for fat intake; in each, fat provides less than 30% of the calories.

In addition to the recipes, we offer practical help in the handy appendix starting on page 100. Here you'll find a glossary of nutrition-related terms, information on interpreting package labels and making lowfat substitutions for familiar foods, and more.

For our recipes, we provide a nutritional analysis (see page 7) prepared by Hill Nutrition Associates, Inc., of Florida. We are grateful to Lynne Hill, R.D., for her advice and expertise.

We thank Rebecca LaBrum for her skillful and careful editing of the manuscript. We also thank Fillamento, R.H., and Forrest Jones for props used in our photographs.

Cover: Minted Lamb Chops & Mushrooms with Pilaf (recipe on page 44) have it all! They're colorful, delicious, low in fat, and delightful for any occasion. Design by Susan Bryant. Photography by Nikolay Zurek. Photo styling by Susan Massey-Weil. Food styling by Cynthia Scheer.

About the Recipes

All of the recipes in this book were tested and developed in the Sunset test kitchens.

*Food and Entertaining Editor,
Sunset Magazine*
Jerry Anne Di Vecchio

Editor, Sunset Books: Elizabeth L. Hogan

First printing January 1992

Contents

Chinese Noodle Salad with Five-spice Chicken (recipe on page 37)

Special Features

Lowfat Cooking

The news is out—lean cooking is in! These days, there's a new outlook on eating. Gone are yesterday's fat- and calorie-laden dishes. In their place are foods that are just as delicious and satisfying, but much better for you: a wealth of fruits and vegetables, tender breads and pastas, lowfat dairy products, and lean meats, poultry, and seafood. Cooking techniques are lighter, too. Today's emphasis is on baking, grilling, roasting, and steaming—methods that go easy on added fats and really enhance the wonderful flavors of fresh foods.

Why change to a lowfat diet? The reason is simply that "old-style" favorites such as deep-fried chicken, well-marbled steaks, and buttery, creamy desserts just aren't appropriate for the way we live. Most of us don't perform the day-long, physically demanding work required to burn the calories such heavy, filling foods provide. And beyond that, we now know that fat-rich diets are linked to high blood pressure, heart disease, obesity, and other health problems.

In the following pages, you'll find all the information you need to make lowfat cooking a natural part of your life. As you'll discover, adjusting your cooking style is easy—and the results couldn't be more flavorful and appealing!

What fats are found in foods?

Food fats are made up of saturated and unsaturated fatty acids; the unsaturated group is further divided into polyunsaturated and monounsaturated kinds. Though food fats contain a mixture of all types of fatty acids, they're classed as saturated, polyunsaturated, or monounsaturated according to the kind present in largest proportion.

Saturated fat is the greatest dietary contributor to increased blood cholesterol. Often solid at room temperature, it's usually found in foods of animal origin: cream, whole milk, whole-milk dairy products such as cheese, butter, and ice cream, and red meats (the fat surrounding and running through meats is saturated). Poultry, fish, and shellfish contain saturated fat in lesser amounts. Saturated fat is also found in some plant products—vegetable fats such as coconut oil, palm kernel oil, palm oil, and cocoa butter, for example. *Hydrogenated* vegetable oils (those that have been converted to solid or semisolid form by the addition of hydrogen) are higher in saturated fat than the unhydrogenated forms. Margarine and vegetable shortening are examples of hydrogenated fats.

Unlike saturated fats, *polyunsaturated* and *monounsaturated* fats are thought to help lower blood cholesterol. Olive and canola (rapeseed) oils are sources of monounsaturated fat; safflower and corn oils are largely polyunsaturated.

What about cholesterol?

Cholesterol, found in all foods of animal origin, is a waxy, odorless, fatlike substance used in the body for the synthesis of vitamins and hormones, the formation of nerve sheaths and cell membranes, and a number of other purposes.

There are two kinds of cholesterol. Some cholesterol, enough for the body's needs, is manufactured in the liver; *dietary cholesterol* comes from the foods we eat. Both types affect your *blood cholesterol level.*

How fats & cholesterol affect your health

An excess of dietary fat—especially saturated fat—is a major cause of heart disease, as well as a contributor to obesity and certain types of cancer. Excess cholesterol is also associated with heart problems: too much dietary cholesterol can result in elevated blood cholesterol, which is linked to heart disease.

The effect of diet on blood cholesterol varies with the individual, but blood cholesterol levels do tend to increase among those whose diets are high in calories, saturated fat, and cholesterol. Of these three factors, dietary saturated fat has the greatest influence on

blood cholesterol, while dietary cholesterol has a lesser effect.

For best health, nutrition experts advise limiting cholesterol intake to 300 milligrams per day. Calories from fat should make up no more than 30% of the day's total (among Americans today, the figure generally ranges from 36% to 42%). It's further recommended that calories from saturated fat should amount to no more than 10% of the daily total—about 20 grams of fat, if you're allowed 2,000 calories per day.

Balancing your diet

The age-old advice is still the best: eat a balanced diet. The hard part is knowing what "balanced" means! Ideally, the foods you eat should provide adequate amounts of all the vital nutrients—not only fat, carbohydrates, and protein, but also vitamins and minerals.

To build a balanced diet, you must eat a variety of foods in moderation. The four food groups you probably learned about in elementary school provide a useful guide (see page 102). Each group is sufficiently varied to allow for plenty of flexibility, enough to design a healthful meatless diet if you wish. You'll find these food groups a useful tool for planning balanced menus such as those on pages 10 through 13.

What about fiber?

So many exaggerated claims have been made about the virtues of dietary fiber (plant material that passes undigested through the intestine) that you may be confused about its actual advantages. In fact, fiber-rich foods do offer some very real health benefits: they help lower blood cholesterol, protect against certain cancers, prevent constipation, and improve the control of blood sugar in diabetics.

Dietary fiber is divided into two groups: soluble and insoluble. Many foods contain both kinds, but one type usually predominates. *Soluble fiber* has been found to lower blood cholesterol levels; the best sources of this sort of fiber are oats, legumes, barley, apples, carrots, and citrus fruits. *Insoluble fiber,* found in wheat bran, whole wheat, other whole grains, fruits, and vegetables, has no known effect on blood cholesterol.

Though the full benefits of fiber are still unknown, health experts recommend a daily consumption of 25 to 35 grams total (both soluble and insoluble). To increase the fiber in your diet, cut back on processed foods and eat more complex carbohydrates, such as whole grains, breads, cereals, fresh fruits, vegetables, and legumes. Ideally, such carbohydrates should

*Made over with lean yogurt and eggless noodles, Light
Chicken Stroganoff (recipe on page 8) is low in fat but every bit
as rich in flavor as the creamy original dish.*

compose about 55% of your total calories. You'll find that complex carbohydrates can help you stick to a lowfat eating plan by providing concentrated energy and giving you a fuller feeling—all for a relatively low calorie count (4 per gram) and a bonus of vitamins and minerals.

Given the heightened interest in fiber, you'll find a wide variety of fiber-rich foods on the market. Just be aware that concentrating on such foods alone won't guarantee you good health; there's no substitute for a balanced diet low in saturated fat and cholesterol. Read ingredient labels carefully (see "How to Read Food Labels," page 106) to make sure the emphasis is on less fat and cholesterol as well as more fiber. Dishes like our Black Bean, Corn & Pepper Salad (page 34) and Apricot Graham Muffins (page 84) are all-around valuable choices for a lowfat, high-fiber diet.

It pays to exercise

Numerous studies have shown that increased physical activity leads to better weight management and improved stamina. Other proven advantages include higher levels of HDL or "good cholesterol" (see "Lipoproteins," page 101), decreased heart disease, reduced blood pressure, and buildup of bone mass (helpful in minimizing the debilitating effects of osteoporosis).

You don't have to be a serious athlete to reap the rewards of exercise. Simply taking a brisk 30- to 60-minute walk three or four times a week provides good aerobic exercise that can condition your heart and lungs. If you plan to embark on a regular vigorous walking program, begin by consulting your doctor if you have heart trouble or a heart murmur, if you have had a heart attack, or if you're over 40 and not accustomed to regular exercise.

When you eat away from home

As the demand for lowfat dishes increases, more and more restaurateurs are responding; in fact, even many fast-food outlets have begun to offer grilled chicken and fish and leaner burgers.

Wherever you're dining—whether at the local pizza palace or an elegant restaurant—learn to scan the menu for lowfat choices. It's often a good idea to call ahead and ask what's offered. You can also find out if the kitchen is willing to accommodate special requests: Will the chef grill meat or poultry instead of frying it? Can rich sauces be omitted or served on the side? When you read a restaurant menu, look for terms that designate lowfat preparation: "grilled," "broiled," "roasted," "poached," "steamed." Likewise, avoid dishes described as "fried," "braised," or "sautéed," as well as those served in sauces you know contain butter, cheese, or cream.

Many restaurants now use special menu symbols to indicate heart-healthy dishes containing a minimum of saturated fat; look for them whenever you eat out. And encourage such establishments by letting your waiter know how much you appreciate these choices.

How to cut fat in cooking

Our recipes make it easy to enjoy a lowfat diet. To start you thinking about entire appetizing meals rich in vegetables, fruits, grains, legumes, and lowfat meats, poultry, and seafood, we've included some tempting menus on pages 10 through 13.

As you'll discover from our recipes, there are certain methods that are best for lowfat cooking: baking, grilling, poaching, steaming, and browning with a bare minimum of oil. Microwaving is another good lowfat cooking technique, since a microwave oven can cook food in its own moisture without added fat. For help in creating lowfat incarnations of your favorite recipes, take a look at our makeovers (pages 8 and 9), substitutions for high-fat ingredients (page 103), and suggestions for lightening traditional dishes (pages 104 and 105).

About our nutritional data

For our recipes, we provide a nutritional analysis stating calorie count; percentage of calories from fat, carbohydrates, and protein; grams of total fat, saturated fat, carbohydrates, and protein; and milligrams of cholesterol and sodium. Generally, the analysis applies to a single serving, based on the number of servings given for each recipe and the amount of each ingredient. If a range is given for the number of servings and/or the amount of an ingredient, the analysis is based on an average of the figures given. The nutritional analysis does not include optional ingredients or those for which no specific amount is stated. If an ingredient is listed with a substitution, the information was calculated using the first choice.

Recipe Makeovers

Switching to a lighter diet doesn't mean giving up all your old favorites. By revising the recipes to use lower fat ingredients and lean cooking methods, you can make a big difference in total fat without greatly changing the flavors you like.

On these pages, we offer original and lighter versions of two main dishes: chicken Stroganoff and a savory meat loaf. Use these examples as models for converting your own treasured recipes.

- *Chicken Stroganoff.* In the original version of this recipe, chicken and vegetables are sautéed in more fat than is really needed. The lighter version browns the chicken strips in a nonstick frying pan coated with a light film of heart-healthy oil; the vegetables soften nicely in the liquid that cooks out of the mushrooms, with very little added oil. Replacing rich sour cream with lowfat yogurt reduces fat and cholesterol considerably. (When you use yogurt in cooking, always remember to stabilize it with a bit of starch; otherwise the heat will cause it to curdle.)

- *Spinach Meat Loaf.* Cheddar cheese—delicious, but high in fat—and a full 2 pounds of ground beef go into the first meat loaf. By substituting a touch of intensely flavored Romano cheese for the Cheddar and replacing half the beef with ground turkey breast, we decrease the total fat appreciably. Boosting the quantity of bread crumbs and mixing in a shredded potato (skin and all) adds valuable carbohydrates—and increases the meat loaf size, too, so it yields more servings. Instead of the original whole eggs, we've used an egg white and evaporated skim milk to bind and moisten the mixture. For a finishing touch, we enlivened the tomato sauce glaze with sweet-tart seasonings. You won't even miss the original topping of melted cheese!

▪ BEFORE

Chicken Stroganoff

½ cup dried tomatoes
¼ cup all-purpose flour
¼ teaspoon pepper
1 pound boneless, skinless chicken breasts, cut into ½-inch cubes
3 tablespoons butter or margarine
3 tablespoons salad oil
1 medium-size onion, chopped
8 ounces mushrooms, sliced
2 cloves garlic, minced or pressed
1 teaspoon cornstarch mixed with 2 teaspoons water
1 cup sour cream
½ cup chicken broth
1 cup dry white wine
½ teaspoon *each* grated fresh ginger and dry thyme
2 tablespoons dry sherry
3 cups hot cooked egg noodles
Chopped parsley

In a bowl, soak tomatoes in hot water to cover until very soft (about 1 hour). Drain well. Chop coarsely; set aside.

In a paper or plastic bag, combine flour and pepper. Shake chicken in bag to coat evenly with flour mixture; shake off excess.

Melt 1½ tablespoons of the butter in 1½ tablespoons of the oil in a wide frying pan over medium-high heat. Add chicken, about half at a time, and cook, stirring often, until no longer pink in center; cut to test (4 to 5 minutes). Remove from pan with a slotted spoon and set aside.

In pan, melt remaining 1½ tablespoons butter in remaining 1½ tablespoons oil. Add onion, mushrooms, and garlic; cook, stirring often, until mushrooms are lightly browned (about 15 minutes). Meanwhile, stir cornstarch mixture into sour cream.

Stir broth, wine, ginger, thyme, and sherry into pan. Bring to a boil, stirring; add tomatoes, chicken, and sour cream mixture. Bring to a boil, stirring. Serve over noodles; sprinkle with parsley. Makes 4 servings.

Per serving: 647 calories (49% fat, 28% carbohydrates, 23% protein), 35 g total fat (15 g saturated fat), 45 g carbohydrates, 37 g protein, 154 mg cholesterol, 331 mg sodium

▪ AFTER

Light Chicken Stroganoff

Pictured on page 6

½ cup dried tomatoes
1 pound boneless, skinless chicken breasts, cut crosswise into ½-inch-wide strips
Ground white pepper
1½ to 2 tablespoons all-purpose flour
1½ tablespoons salad oil
1 medium-size onion, thinly sliced
8 ounces mushrooms, sliced
½ teaspoon *each* grated fresh ginger and dry thyme
4 teaspoons cornstarch mixed with 2 tablespoons water
½ teaspoon sugar
1 cup plain lowfat yogurt
8 ounces medium-wide eggless noodles
2 cloves garlic, minced or pressed
¼ cup low-sodium chicken broth
¾ cup dry white wine
2 tablespoons dry sherry
Chopped parsley

In a small bowl, soak tomatoes in hot water to cover until very soft (about 1 hour). Drain well, cut into strips, and set aside.

Sprinkle chicken with white pepper; dust with flour and shake off excess. Heat 1 tablespoon of the oil in a wide nonstick frying pan over medium-high heat. Add chicken, about half at a time, and cook, lifting and turning often, until lightly browned (4 to 5 minutes). Remove from pan with a slotted spoon and set aside.

When chicken has been cooked, heat remaining 1½ teaspoons oil in pan. Add onion, mushrooms, ginger, and thyme; cook, stirring often, until onion is soft and mush-

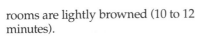

rooms are lightly browned (10 to 12 minutes).

Meanwhile, stir cornstarch mixture and sugar into yogurt and set aside. Also, in a 4½- to 5-quart pan, cook noodles in 2½ quarts boiling water just until tender to bite (about 10 minutes); or cook according to package directions. Drain, then arrange around edge of a warm deep platter; keep warm.

Stir garlic into mushroom mixture and cook for 1 minute. Then stir in broth, wine, and sherry. Bring to a boil, stirring. Add tomatoes, chicken, and yogurt mixture. Bring to a boil, stirring until sauce is thickened. Spoon chicken mixture into center of noodles and sprinkle with parsley. Makes 4 servings.

Per serving: 527 calories (15% fat, 52% carbohydrates, 33% protein), 8 g total fat (2 g saturated fat), 64 g carbohydrates, 41 g protein, 69 mg cholesterol, 159 mg sodium

■ BEFORE

Cheese & Spinach Meat Loaf

- ¾ cup soft bread crumbs
- 2 pounds lean ground beef
- 1 small onion, finely chopped
- 2 eggs, lightly beaten
- 1 can (about 8 oz.) tomato sauce
- 1 teaspoon prepared mustard
- ¾ teaspoon dry oregano
- ½ teaspoon salt
- ¼ teaspoon pepper
- 1 package (about 10 oz.) frozen chopped spinach, thawed and squeezed dry
- 1 teaspoon garlic salt
- 1½ cups (about 6 oz.) shredded sharp Cheddar cheese

In a large bowl, combine crumbs, beef, onion, eggs, ½ cup of the tomato sauce, mustard, oregano, salt, and pepper. On a large sheet of plastic wrap, pat meat mixture into a 12-inch square. Distribute spinach over meat to within ½ inch of edges; sprinkle spinach with garlic salt. Distribute 1 cup of the cheese over spinach to within 1 inch of edges.

Using plastic wrap to lift meat, roll up meat jelly roll style. Pinch seam and ends closed to seal in filling. Carefully place meat roll, seam side down, in a shallow rimmed baking pan.

Bake in a 350° oven for 1¼ hours. Remove pan from oven; spoon out and discard drippings. Pour remaining tomato sauce over meat loaf, return to oven, and continue to bake for 15 more minutes.

Remove meat loaf from oven and sprinkle with remaining ½ cup cheese; return to oven and continue to bake until cheese is melted (about 5 more minutes). With wide spatulas, carefully transfer meat loaf to a warm platter. Let stand for about 5 minutes before slicing. Makes 6 servings.

Per serving: 536 calories (63% fat, 7% carbohydrates, 30% protein), 37 g total fat (17 g saturated fat), 9 g carbohydrates, 40 g protein, 205 mg cholesterol, 1,089 mg sodium

■ AFTER

Leaner Spinach Meat Loaf

- 1 egg white
- ¼ cup evaporated skim milk
- 1 can (about 8 oz.) tomato sauce
- 1½ cups soft French bread crumbs
- 1 small onion, finely chopped
- 1 large potato (about 8 oz.), scrubbed and grated
- 1 clove garlic, minced or pressed
- 2 teaspoons Dijon mustard
- ¾ teaspoon dry oregano
- ¼ teaspoon pepper
- 1 pound extra-lean ground beef
- 1 pound ground skinned turkey breast
- 1 package (about 10 oz.) frozen chopped spinach, thawed and squeezed dry
- ¼ cup grated Romano or Parmesan cheese
- 1 tablespoon *each* firmly packed brown sugar and red wine vinegar
- 1½ teaspoons Worcestershire

In a large bowl, combine egg white, milk, and ½ cup of the tomato sauce; beat until well combined. Stir in crumbs, onion, potato, garlic, mustard, oregano, and pepper. Add beef and turkey; mix lightly. On a large sheet of plastic wrap, pat meat mixture into a 12-inch square. Distribute spinach over meat to within ½ inch of edges; sprinkle evenly with cheese.

Using plastic wrap to lift meat, roll up meat jelly roll style. Pinch seam and ends closed to seal in filling. Carefully place meat roll, seam side down, in a shallow rimmed baking pan.

Bake in a 350° oven for 1¼ hours. Meanwhile, in a small bowl, mix sugar, vinegar, Worcestershire, and remaining tomato sauce; set aside.

Remove pan from oven; spoon out and discard any drippings. Spoon tomato sauce mixture over meat loaf. Return to oven and continue to bake until meat is well browned (15 to 20 more minutes). With wide spatulas, carefully transfer meat loaf to a warm platter. Let stand for about 5 minutes before slicing. Makes 8 servings.

Per serving: 259 calories (28% fat, 27% carbohydrates, 45% protein), 8 g total fat (3 g saturated fat), 17 g carbohydrates, 29 g protein, 72 mg cholesterol, 423 mg sodium

Lowfat Menus for All Seasons

■ Pictured on facing page

Spring Patio Dinner

On a delightfully warm evening in early spring, enjoy this colorful menu for eight to ten. All the foods can easily be carried outdoors. You can bake the fanciful breads and assemble the casserole ahead; you'll need to double the recipe for the papaya dessert.

Vegetable Crudités
Moussaka Dubrovnik (page 53)
Orange & Olive Patio Salad (page 32)
Spring Dove Breads (page 89)
Hot Papaya Sundaes (page 93)
Beaujolais or White Zinfandel
Coffee

Summer Seafood Barbecue

Heat up the grill and prepare a warm-weather treat for seafood lovers only. The tuna recipe yields enough relish for six steaks, but you need only buy four if you're serving a smaller group.

Barbecued Shrimp (page 21)
Grilled Tuna with Tomato-Orange Relish (page 57)
Grilled Multicolored Summer Squash
Wilted Spinach Salad with Oranges (page 33)
Sesame-seed Rolls
Cherries, Berries & French Cream (page 92)
Sauvignon Blanc
Coffee

Autumn Harvest Dinner

This ample meal for six features a cornucopia of bright, wholesome early fall fruits and vegetables. Bake the onion-topped flatbread ahead, then reheat it to enjoy with dinner.

Sweet Potatoes with Caviar (page 20)
Watercress & Pear Salad (page 33)
Garlic Pork Chops with Balsamic Vinegar (page 41)
Noodles
Whole Green Beans
Onion-topped Savory Focaccia (page 87)
Date-stuffed Baked Apples
Zinfandel
Coffee

Wintry Repast

Open this warming supper for eight to ten with mugs of steaming soup while the vegetables and leg of lamb are still roasting in the oven.

Golden Pepper Bisque (page 25)
Gingered Butterflied Lamb with Yams (page 45)
Steamed Broccoli
Crusty Bread
Fresh Winter Pears & Tangerines
Cabernet Sauvignon
Espresso Coffee

Fireside Supper

A savory beef stew is the cozy centerpiece of this hearty meal for four to six. Bake sweet potatoes alongside the stew; prepare the dessert in the oven, too. (You should have enough of the main course left to reheat for a second meal for two to four.)

Potato, Cauliflower & Watercress Soup (page 24)
Crisp Breadsticks
Oven Beef & Mushroom Stew in Bourbon (page 41)
Baked Sweet Potatoes
Steamed Swiss Chard
Rum-drizzled Baked Bananas
Pinot Noir
Coffee

*For a fresh-tasting menu, bring together lightened Moussaka Dubrovnik
(recipe on page 53), bright Orange & Olive Patio Salad (recipe on page 32), and
whimsical Spring Dove Breads (recipe on page 89).*

11

Lowfat Menus for Entertaining

Italian Abbondanza

Festive and abundant, this menu for four to six offers real proof that special meals can be low in fat, yet tops in flavor and appeal.

Roasted Tomato-Eggplant Crostini (page 16)
Watercress, Butter Lettuce & Shrimp Salad (page 32)
Baked Polenta with Veal Sauce (page 42)
Steamed Leaf Spinach
Italian Bread or Rolls
Lemon-tipped Pistachio Biscotti (page 96)
Fresh Fruit
Chianti or Valpolicella
Espresso Coffee

French Bistro Dinner

From the savory first course to the delicate fresh fruit finale, this dinner for eight is genuinely in the spirit of French cooking. You will need to double the recipes for the Brussels sprouts and the raspberries.

Beef Rillettes (page 17)
French Bread & Crisp Romaine Leaves
Hunter's-style Lamb Stew (page 44)
Garlic Potatoes (page 76)
Brussels Sprouts with Mustard Glaze (page 77)
Butter Lettuce with Shallot Dressing (page 36)
Minted Raspberries with White Chocolate (page 92)
Beaujolais or Cabernet Franc
Demitasse Coffee

Southwestern Buffet

Lively flavors from the American Southwest and neighboring Mexico mingle in this colorful help-yourself dinner. The recipes serve six amply.

Chile-rubbed Barbecued Turkey Breast
Black Bean, Corn & Pepper Salad (page 34)
Southwest Blue Cornbread Sticks (page 85)
Amaretti-topped Fresh Pineapple Pie (page 95)
Gewürztraminer
Iced Tea or Coffee

Sultry Weather Supper

Bring a welcome chill to a hot evening with this refreshing menu for four. The noodles are cooked very briefly, then cooled and served at room temperature atop a bed of crisp spinach; the chicken that completes the salad is grilled on the barbecue.

Radishes on Ice
Miniature Crisp Rice Cakes
Chinese Noodle Salad with Five-spice Chicken (page 37)
Ginger-Peach Ice (page 99)
Fortune Cookies
Iced Tea

Farmers' Market Barbecue

After you've shopped at an outdoor market or roadside stand, bring your treasures home and create this luscious meal for six.

Melon Wedges with Lime
Grilled Beef & Peppers with Orzo (page 40)
Corn on the Cob
Shredded Zucchini Salad with Green Chile Dressing (page 36)
Orange Blossom Strawberry Pie (page 96)
Lemonade
Light Red Wine
Coffee

Quick Lowfat Menus

Fall Chicken Dinner

For family fare, consider this spicy and colorful chicken dinner for four to six. Steam the rice and assemble the salad while the chicken is simmering.

Apple Country Chicken (page 48)
Fluffy White or Brown Rice
Red & Green Cabbage Salad with Garlic Buttermilk Dressing (page 36)
Grape Clusters
Milk
Coffee

Friday Night Pasta

You'll find this menu for four a speedy choice for spur-of-the-moment entertaining. Serve it in summer or early autumn, when the plump Roma tomatoes for the uncooked pasta sauce are at their fresh best.

Halibut with Tomato-Cilantro Linguine (page 56)
Mixed Green Salad with Green Chile Dressing (page 36)
Crusty Rolls
Frozen Yogurt with Sliced Nectarines
Pinot Gris or Sauvignon Blanc

Family Soup Supper

This hearty soup is so full of vegetables, pasta, and ground turkey that it's virtually a meal in one pot or tureen. You'll have six to eight ample servings; leftovers make a good lowfat lunch.

Harvest Turkey Soup (page 29)
Soft Breadsticks
Green Apple & Butter Lettuce Salad
Peach & Raspberry Crisp (page 93)
Cider or Light Red Wine

Speedy Stir-fry

Quick but quite elegant, this pairing of grilled chicken and stir-fried vegetables can be assembled at the last minute—but you'll need to prepare the frozen chocolate dessert in advance. The menu serves four, with two extra tartufi.

Sesame Chicken with Stir-fried Vegetables (page 50)
Fluffy Rice
Olive Rolls or Bread
Frozen Italian Chocolate Tartufi (page 99)
Sauvignon Blanc or Dry Chenin Blanc
Coffee

Burgers in a Basket

Serve this tempting family supper for six informally, in front of the television set or on the patio.

Turkey & Mushroom Burgers on Onion Rolls (page 52)
Tomatoes, Mustard, Lettuce & Pickles
Garlic Potatoes (page 76)
Watermelon Wedges
Soft Drinks or Nonfat Milk
Beer

For a distinctive beginning to a casual company meal, try Chinese
Corn Crêpes with Grilled Pork (recipe on page 20): warm, cornmeal-crunchy
griddlecakes wrapped around slivered green onions, spicy hoisin sauce,
and thinly sliced marinated pork. Pour cold, frothy Chinese beer or tall
glasses of iced tea to sip alongside these tasty appetizers.

Appetizers

Whether you're giving a dinner party or just sharing a glass of wine with friends, the occasion is more festive when a well-chosen appetizer is at hand. Let the good times begin with crisp morsels and savory nibbles hot or cold, all designed to be both low in fat and high in nutritional value.

There's a wider range of lowfat appetizers than you may have imagined. You can enjoy virtually the entire spectrum of colorful vegetables, either crunchy and raw—as in Black Bean Salsa & Crisp Vegetables—or baked to melting tenderness, as in Roasted Tomato-Eggplant Crostini. When you hunger for something a bit more substantial, snack on lean meats or seafood: savory Beef Rillettes on crusty baguette slices, or skewered Apricot-Orange Glazed Chicken or Barbecued Shrimp served sizzling-hot from the grill.

Whatever your taste, make your appetizer selections from lowfat foods that are also high in vitamins, minerals, and fiber. And try to keep the calorie count and sodium level down, too. For variety, choose from all four food groups (see page 102): vegetables and fruits, lowfat and non-fat dairy products, whole-grain breads and crackers made with a minimum of fat (preferably an unsaturated vegetable oil), and nibbling-size portions of lean meat, poultry, fish, and shellfish.

Roasted Tomato-Eggplant Crostini

Preparation time: About 15 minutes

Cooking time: About 54 minutes

Meals in Italy often begin with *crostini*—bread or toast with a savory spread. Our lowfat topping combines red onion, tomatoes, and eggplant, baked until almost charred to caramelize their natural sugars.

Olive oil cooking spray

1 large red onion (about 12 oz.), cut into ½-inch-thick slices

2 tablespoons balsamic or red wine vinegar

1½ pounds firm-ripe pear-shaped (Roma-type) tomatoes (about 8 large), cut into ¼-inch-thick slices

1 medium-size eggplant (about 1 lb.), unpeeled, cut crosswise into ½-inch-thick slices

Salt and pepper

16 slices crusty Italian or French bread (*each about 3½ inches wide, 5 inches long, and ½ inch thick*)

Spray two 10- by 15-inch rimmed baking pans with cooking spray. Arrange onion slices in a single layer in one of the pans; drizzle with vinegar. Arrange tomato slices in same pan, overlapping slightly. Arrange eggplant slices in a single layer in second pan. Spray all vegetables lightly with cooking spray. Bake in a 450° oven until eggplant is browned and very soft when pressed (about 30 minutes) and tomatoes are well browned on edges (about 50 minutes).

Transfer all vegetables to a food processor or blender; whirl until coarsely puréed. Season to taste with salt and pepper.

Place bread in a single layer on a baking sheet. Broil about 5 inches below heat, turning once, until golden on both sides (about 4 minutes).

To serve, spread toast with vegetable purée, using about 2 tablespoons per slice. Makes 16 appetizers.

Per appetizer: 91 calories (14% fat, 74% carbohydrates, 12% protein), 1 g total fat (0.2 g saturated fat), 17 g carbohydrates, 3 g protein, 0.7 mg cholesterol, 133 mg sodium

Corn Relish & Water-crisped Tortilla Chips

Preparation time: About 20 minutes

Cooking time: About 11 minutes

Serve this green-and-gold relish as a dip for crisp corn or flour tortilla chips or as an accompaniment for grilled meat or chicken.

Water-crisped Tortilla Chips (recipe follows)

3 medium-size ears corn

½ cup finely chopped English cucumber

⅓ cup lime juice

¼ cup thinly sliced green onions

1 tablespoon grated orange peel

3 tablespoons orange juice

2 tablespoons chopped fresh mint or 1 teaspoon dry mint

1 teaspoon cumin seeds

1 or 2 small fresh jalapeño chiles, seeded and finely chopped

Salt

Prepare Water-crisped Tortilla Chips and set aside.

Discard husks and silk from corn. In a 5- to 6-quart pan, bring about 3 quarts water to a boil over high heat. Add corn, cover, and cook until hot (about 5 minutes). Drain and let cool; cut kernels from cobs.

In a medium-size bowl, mix corn, cucumber, lime juice, onions, orange peel, orange juice, mint, cumin seeds, and chiles. Season to taste with salt. If made ahead, cover and refrigerate for up to a day. Serve relish with tortilla chips. Makes 12 servings.

■ *Water-crisped Tortilla Chips.* Dip 12 **corn or flour tortillas** (*each* 6 or 7 inches in diameter), one at a time, in **water;** let drain briefly. Season to taste with **salt.** Stack tortillas; cut stack into 6 or 8 wedges. Spread out wedges in a single layer on large baking sheets. Bake in a 500° oven for 4 minutes. Turn wedges over; continue to bake until browned and crisp (about 2 more minutes). If made ahead, let cool; store airtight at room temperature for up to 1 week. Makes 12 servings.

Per serving: 93 calories (13% fat, 75% carbohydrates, 12% protein), 1 g total fat (0 g saturated fat), 19 g carbohydrates, 3 g protein, 0 mg cholesterol, 58 mg sodium

Black Bean Salsa & Crisp Vegetables

Preparation time: About 25 minutes

Canned black beans seasoned with fresh lime juice, cilantro, green onions, and tomatoes make a quick, satisfying dip. Present the savory mixture with crisp cucumber and jicama slices.

- 1 can (about 15 oz.) black beans
- 2 tablespoons lime juice
- ⅓ cup coarsely chopped cilantro
- ½ cup thinly sliced green onions
- 3 small pear-shaped (Roma-type) tomatoes (about 6 oz. *total*), seeded and chopped

    Salt and pepper
- 1 small jicama (about 1 lb.)
- 1 small English cucumber (about 10 oz.), thinly sliced

    Cilantro sprigs

Drain beans, reserving 1 tablespoon of the liquid. Place reserved liquid and half the beans in a medium-size bowl. Add lime juice, then mash beans with a fork or potato masher until smooth. Stir in remaining beans, chopped cilantro, onions, and tomatoes. Season to taste with salt and pepper. If made ahead, cover and refrigerate for up to 4 hours.

Peel and rinse jicama; cut in half lengthwise, then thinly slice each half. Arrange jicama and cucumber slices on a platter and set aside. If made ahead, cover and refrigerate for up to 2 hours.

Spoon bean mixture into a serving bowl; garnish with cilantro sprigs. Offer to spoon onto jicama and cucumber slices to taste. Makes about 30 servings.

Per serving: 57 calories (4% fat, 73% carbohydrates, 23% protein), 0.2 g total fat (0.1 g saturated fat), 11 g carbohydrates, 3 g protein, 0 mg cholesterol, 2 mg sodium

Beef Rillettes

Preparation time: About 25 minutes

Baking time: About 4 hours

Chilling time: At least 7 hours

Rillettes, an appetizer spread popular in the Loire Valley of France, is usually made from succulent pork cooked and preserved in its own fat. Our lower-fat version of this treat uses naturally lean beef shanks, oven-braised until very tender; the softly jelled cooking juices moisten the mixture pleasantly.

- About 1¼ pounds beef shanks (about 1 inch thick)
- 1 clove garlic
- ½ teaspoon *each* pepper and dry thyme
- 1 bay leaf
- 2 cups water

    Salt
- 2 small French bread baguettes (about 8 oz. *each*), thinly sliced
- 2 heads Belgian endive (about 6 oz. *total*), separated into spears, rinsed, and crisped (optional)

    Dijon mustard (optional)

Place beef in a 1¼- to 1½-quart casserole; add garlic, pepper, thyme, and bay leaf. Pour in water; cover tightly and bake in a 250° oven until meat is so tender it falls apart in shreds when prodded with a fork (about 4 hours).

Lift beef from casserole, reserving liquid. Let beef stand until cool enough to touch; then pull off and discard all fat, bones, and connective tissue. Tear meat into fine shreds, cover, and refrigerate. Refrigerate cooking liquid separately until surface fat has hardened (about 4 hours).

Lift off and discard fat from liquid. Measure liquid (it should be softly jelled); you need 1½ cups. If liquid is still fluid, boil until reduced to 1½ cups; if it is rigid, add water to make 1½ cups. Heat liquid until hot; add meat and heat until warm. Season to taste with salt. Pour into a 2½- to 3-cup crock or jar. Cover and refrigerate until firm (at least 3 hours) or for up to 3 days (gelatin may weep if mixture is kept longer).

To serve, spread rillettes on bread slices or, if desired, spoon into endive spears. Add mustard to taste, if desired. Makes about 2¼ cups.

Per tablespoon serving on bread: 51 calories (14% fat, 58% carbohydrates, 28% protein), 0.8 g total fat (0.2 g saturated fat), 7 g carbohydrates, 3 g protein, 5 mg cholesterol, 80 mg sodium

■ Pictured on facing page

Swordfish with Lemon Relish

Preparation time: About 30 minutes

Cooking time: 35 to 40 minutes

These canapé-style appetizers are a refreshing choice for a stand-up cocktail party. Toasted baguette slices are topped with a sweet-tart lemon relish, squares of meaty swordfish, and thin tomato strips.

Lemon Peel Relish (recipe follows)

32 **French bread baguette slices (*each* about 2 inches wide and ¼ inch thick)**

1 **pound boneless, skinless swordfish steaks (about ½ inch thick)**

¼ **cup dry white wine**

Salt and pepper

2 **small pear-shaped (Roma-type) tomatoes (about 4 oz. *total*), seeded and cut into thin strips**

Parsley sprigs

Prepare Lemon Peel Relish.

Arrange bread slices in a single layer on baking sheets. Bake in a 350° oven until lightly toasted (about 10 minutes). Let cool.

Rinse fish, pat dry, and cut into 16 equal pieces, each about 1 inch square. Then cut each piece in half horizontally so that pieces are about ¼ inch thick. Arrange fish in a single layer in a foil-lined 10- by 15-inch rimmed baking pan. Drizzle with wine; season to taste with salt and pepper. Cover loosely with foil.

Bake in a 375° oven until fish is just opaque but still moist in center; cut to test (about 6 minutes). Let cool in pan. (At this point, you may cover and refrigerate for up to 4 hours.)

Up to 30 minutes before serving, spoon equal amounts of Lemon Peel Relish onto each bread slice. Just before serving, drain fish and pat dry; set a piece atop relish on each bread slice. Top with tomatoes and parsley sprigs. Makes 32 appetizers.

■ *Lemon Peel Relish.* With a vegetable peeler, pare yellow peel (including a little white pith) from 6 large **lemons.** Mince peel. Cut off and discard remaining pith from 2 of the lemons (reserve remaining 4 lemons for other uses). Cut the 2 lemons into chunks; remove and discard seeds. Chop fruit coarsely.

Heat 1 tablespoon **salad oil** in a medium-size frying pan over medium-high heat. Add ½ cup finely chopped **onion;** cook, stirring often, until onion is soft but not browned (3 to 5 minutes). Add lemon peel, chopped lemons, ½ cup **dry white wine,** ⅓ cup **sugar,** and 1 teaspoon **pepper.** Cook, stirring often, until almost all liquid has cooked away and mixture is syrupy (15 to 18 minutes). Let cool.

Per appetizer: 56 calories (19% fat, 55% carbohydrates, 26% protein), 1 g total fat (0.2 g saturated fat), 8 g carbohydrates, 4 g protein, 6 mg cholesterol, 57 mg sodium

■ Pictured on facing page

Roasted Potatoes Parmesan

Preparation time: About 15 minutes

Baking time: About 1¼ hours

Tiny red-skinned potatoes—sometimes sold as "creamers"—are baked, split, and crowned with a tempting topping of Parmesan and tangy yogurt.

16 **small red thin-skinned potatoes (*each* 1½ to 2 inches in diameter), scrubbed**

⅓ **cup *each* grated Parmesan cheese and plain lowfat yogurt**

2 **tablespoons minced green onion or chives**

Paprika

Pierce each potato in several places with a fork. Arrange in a single layer in a shallow baking pan.

Bake in a 375° oven until tender when pierced (about 1 hour). Let cool slightly. (At this point, you may cover and refrigerate for up to a day.)

In a small bowl, mix cheese, yogurt, and onion.

To fill potatoes, cut each in half. Scoop out a small depression from center of cut side of each potato half. Set halves, cut sides up, in a shallow rimmed baking pan (if necessary, trim a sliver from rounded side of potato halves to steady them). Spoon cheese mixture into potato halves. Sprinkle generously with paprika. Bake in a 350° oven until heated through (about 15 minutes). Serve hot. Makes 32 appetizers.

Per appetizer: 23 calories (12% fat, 72% carbohydrates, 16% protein), 0.3 g total fat (0.2 g saturated fat), 4 g carbohydrates, 1 g protein, 0.8 mg cholesterol, 19 mg sodium

Start off a summer patio party with a pair of lowfat nibbles: hot Roasted Potatoes Parmesan and cool, colorful Swordfish with Lemon Relish (recipes on facing page). Both are perfect finger foods, easy to pick up and neat to eat.

Sweet Potatoes with Caviar

Preparation time: About 15 minutes

Baking time: About 25 minutes

Crisp-baked sweet potato slices are a delectable base for sour cream and crunchy golden caviar. Use inexpensive caviar, such as flying fish roe *(tobiko)*, crab roe *(masago)*, or lumpfish, whitefish, or salmon caviar.

> 2 **pounds sweet potatoes (*each* about 2 inches in diameter), scrubbed**
> **Vegetable oil cooking spray**
> ¼ **cup caviar**
> ⅓ **to ½ cup light sour cream**

Cut off and discard ends of unpeeled potatoes, then cut potatoes crosswise into ¼-inch-thick slices. Spray two 10- by 15-inch rimmed baking pans with cooking spray. Arrange potato slices in a single layer in pans. Spray with cooking spray.

Bake in a 400° oven until slices are golden brown on bottom (about 15 minutes); turn slices over and continue to bake until browned on top (about 10 more minutes). Potatoes at edges of pans brown faster, so move these to centers of pans when you turn slices.

While potatoes are baking, place caviar in a fine wire strainer and rinse under cool running water; drain well, then refrigerate until ready to use.

Lift potato slices onto a platter in a single layer. Dot each with sour cream, then with caviar. Serve hot or warm. Makes about 60 appetizers.

Per appetizer: 18 calories (27% fat, 61% carbohydrates, 12% protein), 1 g total fat (0.1 g saturated fat), 3 g carbohydrates, 1 g protein, 7 mg cholesterol, 17 mg sodium

■ *Pictured on page 14*

Chinese Corn Crêpes with Grilled Pork

Preparation time: About 10 minutes, plus at least 30 minutes to marinate meat

Cooking time: About 50 minutes

In northern China, dried and ground corn is used to make *jian bin*—crisp-chewy, crêpelike griddlecakes. Here, they're wrapped around thinly sliced barbecued pork for a savory appetizer.

> **Grilled Pork (recipe follows)**
> **Chinese Corn Crêpes (recipe follows)**
> **About ⅓ cup hoisin sauce**
> **About ½ cup slivered green onions**

Marinate Grilled Pork. Prepare crêpes.

Barbecue pork. Meanwhile, wrap stacked crêpes in foil and reheat in a 350° oven until warm (about 15 minutes). To serve, cut pork into thin slices. Wrap pork in crêpes, adding hoisin sauce and onions to taste. Makes 12 to 14 servings.

■ *Grilled Pork.* In a shallow bowl, mix 1 clove **garlic** (minced or pressed), ¼ teaspoon **crushed red pepper flakes**, 1 teaspoon **Chinese five-spice powder** (or ½ teaspoon *each* ground ginger and cinnamon), 1 tablespoon **soy sauce**, 2 teaspoons **salad oil**, and 2 tablespoons **rice vinegar**. Trim 1 **pork tenderloin** (about 12 oz.) of fat and silvery membrane. Add pork to marinade; turn to coat. Cover and refrigerate for at least 30 minutes or up to 3 hours, turning several times.

Lift pork from bowl, reserving marinade. Place on a lightly greased grill 4 to 6 inches above a solid bed of medium-hot coals. Cook, brushing with marinade and turning 2 or 3 times to brown all sides, until a meat thermometer inserted in thickest part registers 155°F (about 20 minutes). Lift to a carving board and keep warm for about 5 minutes before slicing.

■ *Chinese Corn Crêpes.* In a blender, whirl until blended 1¾ cups plus 2 tablespoons **water;** 1 cup **yellow cornmeal;** ½ cup **all-purpose flour;** 1 teaspoon **salad oil;** and ¼ teaspoon **salt**. Spray a 6- to 7-inch crêpe pan with **vegetable oil cooking spray;** heat pan over medium heat until a drop of water dances on surface. To cook each crêpe, pour 3 tablespoons batter into pan; tilt so batter covers entire surface. Cook until top of crêpe is dry. Carefully turn crêpe and brown other side; then turn out onto a plate. Stack crêpes as made. Use more cooking spray as needed to prevent sticking; stir batter often to keep cornmeal from settling.

Per serving: 114 calories (21% fat, 51% carbohydrates, 28% protein), 3 g total fat (0.5 g saturated fat), 14 g carbohydrates, 8 g protein, 19 mg cholesterol, 323 mg sodium

Apricot-Orange Glazed Chicken

Preparation time: About 15 minutes, plus at least 30 minutes to soak skewers

Broiling time: About 8 minutes

An easy apricot jam sauce spiked with horseradish and ginger gives this lean grilled chicken-on-a-stick its luscious flavor.

> 6 **boneless, skinless chicken breast halves (about 2 lbs. *total*)**
>
> 1 **cup apricot jam**
>
> 2 **tablespoons *each* prepared horseradish, minced fresh ginger, grated orange peel, and firmly packed brown sugar**
>
> ¼ **cup orange juice**

Soak 36 bamboo skewers (6 to 8 inches long) in hot water to cover for at least 30 minutes.

Rinse chicken and pat dry. Cut each piece lengthwise into 6 equal slices, then weave each slice onto a skewer. Place skewers on a lightly greased rack in a broiling pan.

In a 1- to 1½-quart pan, combine jam, horseradish, ginger, orange peel, sugar, and orange juice. Stir over medium-high heat until jam is melted; keep mixture warm.

Brush chicken with some of the jam mixture. Broil 6 inches below heat, turning once and brushing 2 or 3 times with remaining jam mixture, until meat in thickest part is no longer pink; cut to test (about 8 minutes). Brush with any remaining jam mixture, then serve hot. Makes 36 appetizers.

Per appetizer: 52 calories (9% fat, 56% carbohydrates, 35% protein), 1 g total fat (0.1 g saturated fat), 7 g carbohydrates, 5 g protein, 12 mg cholesterol, 13 mg sodium

Barbecued Shrimp

Preparation time: About 25 minutes, plus at least 4 hours to marinate shrimp

Cooking time: About 4 minutes

First marinated in a sweet-sharp tomato sauce, then threaded on bamboo skewers, these succulent shrimp can be grilled or broiled.

> 1 **can (about 8 oz.) tomato sauce**
>
> ½ **cup light molasses**
>
> 1 **teaspoon dry mustard**
>
> **Dash of liquid hot pepper seasoning**
>
> 1 **clove garlic, minced or pressed**
>
> 1 **tablespoon salad oil**
>
> ⅛ **teaspoon dry thyme**
>
> **Freshly ground pepper**
>
> 2 **pounds medium-size raw shrimp (40 to 45 per lb.), shelled and deveined**

In a large glass bowl, mix tomato sauce, molasses, mustard, hot pepper seasoning, garlic, oil, and thyme. Season to taste with pepper. Add shrimp and stir to coat. Cover and refrigerate for at least 4 hours or until next day.

While shrimp are marinating, soak about 24 bamboo skewers (6 to 8 inches long) in hot water to cover for at least 30 minutes.

Lift shrimp from bowl, reserving marinade; thread 3 or 4 shrimp on each skewer. Place on a lightly greased grill about 6 inches above a solid bed of low coals. (Or place on a rimmed baking sheet and broil about 6 inches below heat.) Cook, turning once and brushing often with marinade, just until shrimp are opaque in center; cut to test (about 4 minutes). Makes about 24 appetizers.

Per appetizer: 41 calories (16% fat, 21% carbohydrates, 63% protein), 1 g total fat (0.1 g saturated fat), 2 g carbohydrates, 6 g protein, 47 mg cholesterol, 65 mg sodium

Brimming with vegetables and tidbits of ground turkey, savory Harvest Turkey Soup (recipe on page 29) is a full meal that's rich in flavor—but low in fat. Complete a nourishing cold-weather supper with chewy breadsticks and a light red wine or apple cider.

Soups

Generations of resourceful cooks have been admired for their skill in transforming commonplace foods into uncommonly delicious dishes. Intricately flavored soups, wafting clouds of aromatic steam, are one hallmark of such culinary ingenuity. Surprisingly, their superb taste needn't come at the cost of good nutrition; by combining seasonal vegetables with grains, pasta, lean dairy products, seafood, and poultry, you can create lowfat soups that seem marvelously rich.

Versatile vegetable purées such as Potato, Cauliflower & Watercress Soup and Golden Pepper Bisque introduce multicourse dinners elegantly—and also make a fine, simple lunch or supper with the addition of a plump loaf of crusty bread. Likewise, vivid Red Onion Borscht is equally good as a light main course or as the opener for an herbed stew or other hearty entrée.

Main-dish soups hold the same appeal for hurried cooks as do casseroles, offering a virtually complete meal from one pot. Happily, ample choices such as creamy Crab & Rice Chowder and chunky Harvest Turkey Soup also go together in very little time.

When our recipes call for broth, we've specified a low-sodium variety. Look for low-salt, richly flavored canned broth; or make your own (see page 105) to keep on hand in the freezer.

Warm-up Vegetable Soup

Preparation time: 25 minutes

Cooking time: About 40 minutes

Start off a casual supper with bowls of this comforting fresh vegetable soup. Steaming, herb-scented chicken broth holds tender pasta shells and a colorful medley of mushrooms, potato chunks, banana squash, and diced tomatoes.

1 tablespoon olive oil or salad oil

1 medium-size onion, finely chopped

8 ounces mushrooms, thinly sliced

1 teaspoon *each* dry oregano, dry basil, and dry marjoram

6 cups low-sodium chicken broth

1 medium-size thin-skinned potato (about 6 oz.), peeled and cut into ½-inch cubes

1 pound banana squash, peeled and cut into ½-inch cubes

¾ cup small or medium-size dry pasta shells

1 cup diced pear-shaped (Roma-type) tomatoes

Salt and pepper

Heat oil in a 5- to 6-quart pan over medium heat. Add onion, mushrooms, oregano, basil, and marjoram. Cook, stirring often, until vegetables are tinged with brown (about 10 minutes). Stir in broth, potato, and squash. Bring to a boil; reduce heat, cover, and boil gently until potato is tender to bite (about 15 minutes).

Add pasta, cover, and continue to cook until pasta is just tender to bite (about 8 more minutes). Stir in tomatoes and heat through (about 2 minutes). Season to taste with salt and pepper. Makes 6 servings.

Per serving: 159 calories (25% fat, 59% carbohydrates, 16% protein), 4 g total fat (0.8 g saturated fat), 24 g carbohydrates, 7 g protein, 0 mg cholesterol, 62 mg sodium

Potato, Cauliflower & Watercress Soup

Preparation time: About 20 minutes

Cooking time: 35 to 40 minutes

A generous measure of fresh watercress lightens this sturdy blend of two winter vegetables—and adds a peppery jolt of flavor. Topped with tart yogurt, cups of the smooth-textured soup make a satisfying opener for a cold-weather meal.

1½ cups cauliflower flowerets, cut into bite-size pieces

2½ cups nonfat milk

2 tablespoons margarine

½ cup slivered shallots

⅛ teaspoon ground nutmeg

2 large russet potatoes (about 1 lb. *total*), peeled and diced

1¾ cups low-sodium chicken broth

2 bunches watercress (about 12 oz. *total*), rinsed, drained, and torn into sprigs (about 2 quarts, lightly packed)

Salt and freshly ground white pepper

¼ to ⅓ cup plain lowfat yogurt or light sour cream

In a 2- to 3-quart pan, combine cauliflower and milk. Bring to a boil over medium heat; reduce heat to medium-low and cook until cauliflower is tender when pierced (8 to 10 minutes). Place a strainer over a large bowl and pour cauliflower mixture through it; set cauliflower and milk aside separately.

Rinse pan; set over medium heat and add margarine. When margarine is melted, add shallots and nutmeg; cook, stirring occasionally, until shallots are soft but not browned (3 to 5 minutes). Add potatoes and broth; increase heat to medium-high and bring to a boil. Reduce heat, cover, and simmer until potatoes are very tender when pierced (about 10 minutes). Reserve several watercress sprigs for garnish, then stir remaining watercress into potato mixture and cook, uncovered, for 5 minutes. Add cauliflower to pan and cook until heated through (about 3 minutes).

In a blender or food processor, whirl potato mixture, half at a time, until smooth. Return to pan, add reserved milk, and heat just until steaming (do not boil). Season to taste with salt and white pepper. Garnish each serving with a dollop of yogurt and a watercress sprig. Makes 4 to 6 servings.

Per serving: 201 calories (26% fat, 54% carbohydrates, 20% protein), 6 g total fat (1 g saturated fat), 28 g carbohydrates, 10 g protein, 3 mg cholesterol, 192 mg sodium

Golden Pepper Bisque

Preparation time: About 20 minutes, plus 30 minutes to cool peppers

Cooking time: 1 to 1¼ hours

Cooked until very soft, then puréed, thin-skinned potatoes lend a silky texture to this distinctive golden soup. Topped with crisp croutons and a sprinkling of Parmesan cheese, it's a memorable first course.

    French Bread Croutons (recipe follows)
2   large yellow bell peppers (about 1 lb. *total*)
1   tablespoon olive oil or salad oil
1   large onion, chopped
2   large thin-skinned potatoes (about 1 lb. *total*), peeled and diced
2   large carrots (about 8 oz. *total*), cut into ½-inch-thick slices
1   large stalk celery, thinly sliced
6   cups low-sodium chicken broth
    Salt and pepper
    Grated Parmesan cheese (optional)

Prepare French Bread Croutons.

Place bell peppers in a 9-inch baking pan and broil about 4 inches below heat, turning as needed, until charred on all sides (15 to 20 minutes). Cover with foil; let cool for 30 minutes. Remove and discard stems, skins, and seeds; rinse peppers and chop coarsely.

Heat oil in a 4- to 5-quart pan over medium-high heat. Add onion and cook, stirring occasionally, until it begins to brown (about 5 minutes). Add bell peppers, potatoes, carrots, celery, and broth. Bring to a boil; reduce heat, cover, and boil gently until carrots are very soft to bite (20 to 25 minutes).

In a blender or food processor, whirl vegetable mixture, about a third at a time, until smoothly puréed. Return all purée to pan; cook over medium heat, stirring often, until heated through. Season to taste with salt and pepper. Sprinkle croutons over each portion. Serve with cheese to add to taste, if desired. Makes 6 to 8 servings.

▪ *French Bread Croutons.* Spray a shallow rimmed baking pan with **olive oil cooking spray**. Spread 4 cups ¾-inch cubes **French bread** (about 4 oz.) in pan. Spray bread cubes with cooking spray. Bake in a 350° oven until crisp and golden brown (12 to 15 minutes). If made ahead, let cool in pan on a rack; then store airtight at room temperature for up to 2 days.

Per serving: 174 calories (22% fat, 65% carbohydrates, 13% protein), 4 g total fat (0.7 g saturated fat), 29 g carbohydrates, 6 g protein, 0.5 mg cholesterol, 163 mg sodium

Sweet Potato Soup

Preparation time: About 20 minutes

Cooking time: About 25 minutes

Despite their rich flavor, sweet potatoes contain no more calories by weight than thin-skinned potatoes or russets. This smooth sweet potato purée, accented with curry and sherry, makes a sophisticated starter for a special meal.

4   medium-large sweet potatoes or yams (about 3 lbs. *total*), peeled and diced
      About 6 cups low-sodium chicken broth
1½   tablespoons curry powder
¼   cup tomato paste
2   tablespoons lemon juice
¼   cup dry sherry
      Salt and pepper
      Cilantro leaves

In a 4- to 5-quart pan, combine potatoes and 6 cups of the broth. Bring to a boil over medium-high heat; reduce heat, cover, and boil gently until potatoes are soft enough to mash readily (about 20 minutes). With a slotted spoon, transfer potatoes to a food processor or blender; add curry powder and about ½ cup of the cooking broth. Whirl until puréed.

Return sweet potato purée to pan; stir in tomato paste, lemon juice, and sherry. If made ahead, cover and refrigerate for up to a day.

To serve, reheat soup over medium heat, stirring often, until hot. If soup is too thick, thin with a little more broth. Season to taste with salt and pepper. Garnish with cilantro. Makes 8 to 10 servings.

Per serving: 148 calories (9% fat, 81% carbohydrates, 10% protein), 2 g total fat (0.3 g saturated fat), 30 g carbohydrates, 4 g protein, 0 mg cholesterol, 109 mg sodium

Red Onion Borscht

Preparation time: About 15 minutes

Cooking time: 40 to 45 minutes

Traditional dishes are often rich, too—but this flavorful borscht is low in both fat and calories. Slow cooking brings out the natural sweetness of red onions, while shredded beets intensify their vivid color. Try cups of the soup as a lead-in to lean braised brisket or another hearty main course.

  1½ **tablespoons salad oil**
  4 **large red onions (2½ to 3 lbs.** *total)***, thinly sliced**
  ½ **cup red wine vinegar**
  2 **medium-size beets (8 to 10 oz.** *total)***, peeled and shredded**
  2½ **tablespoons all-purpose flour**
  6 **cups low-sodium chicken broth**
  ⅓ **cup port**
    Salt and pepper
    Light sour cream (optional)

Heat oil in a 5- to 6-quart pan over medium-low heat. Add onions, vinegar, and beets. Cook, stirring often, until onions are very soft but not browned (25 to 30 minutes). Add flour and stir until bubbly. Remove pan from heat and gradually stir in broth. (At this point, you may cover and refrigerate for up to 2 days.)

Return soup to medium heat and bring to a boil, stirring occasionally; then reduce heat and simmer for 10 minutes. Stir in port. Season to taste with salt and pepper. Garnish each serving with sour cream, if desired. Makes 8 servings.

Per serving: 215 calories (29% fat, 58% carbohydrates, 13% protein), 7 g total fat (1 g saturated fat), 29 g carbohydrates, 7 g protein, 0 mg cholesterol, 96 mg sodium

Crab & Rice Chowder

Preparation time: About 15 minutes

Cooking time: 20 to 25 minutes

Bright bell pepper, broccoli, and corn help extend less than half a pound of crabmeat into a satisfying main-dish soup for six. To complete a wholesome supper, just add a loaf of crusty bread.

  1 **tablespoon salad oil**
  1 **small onion, finely chopped**
  8 **ounces mushrooms, thinly sliced**
  ½ **teaspoon dry thyme**
  2 **cups coarsely chopped broccoli flowerets**
  1 **small red bell pepper (about 5 oz.), seeded and finely chopped**
  2 **cups low-sodium chicken broth**
  2 **cups lowfat milk**
  1 **can (about 17 oz.) cream-style corn**
  6 **ounces cooked crabmeat**
  3 **cups cooked long-grain white rice**
    Salt and pepper

Heat oil in a 4- to 5-quart pan over medium-high heat. Add onion, mushrooms, and thyme; cook, stirring often, until vegetables begin to brown (about 8 minutes). Add broccoli and bell pepper; cook, stirring often, until broccoli turns bright green and begins to soften (about 4 minutes).

Stir in broth, milk, and corn; cook just until heated through, but do not boil (5 to 7 minutes). Stir in crab and rice; again, cook just until heated through (2 to 3 minutes). Season to taste with salt and pepper. Makes 6 servings.

Per serving: 317 calories (16% fat, 65% carbohydrates, 19% protein), 6 g total fat (2 g saturated fat), 53 g carbohydrates, 15 g protein, 35 mg cholesterol, 377 mg sodium

Vivid in color and intense in flavor, Red Onion Borscht (recipe on facing page) makes a striking first course. Or serve it as a main dish, along with thickly sliced whole-grain bread and a selection of ripe fresh fruit. Top each bright bowlful with a creamy dollop of light sour cream, if you like.

Asparagus, Shrimp & Watercress Soup

Preparation time: About 20 minutes

Cooking time: About 10 minutes

There's more than a hint of spring in this light main-course soup. Each bowlful brings together vivid green watercress, blushing pink shrimp, and delicate strands of pasta. Serve with seeded breadsticks and a crisp white wine, such as Pinot Grigio.

12	ounces asparagus
7	cups low-sodium chicken broth
1	teaspoon *each* grated lemon peel and dry tarragon
⅛	teaspoon ground white pepper
1	ounce dry capellini or coil vermicelli
12	ounces medium-size raw shrimp (40 to 45 per lb.), shelled and deveined
2	cups lightly packed watercress sprigs, rinsed and drained
3	tablespoons lemon juice

Snap off and discard tough ends of asparagus, then cut spears into ½-inch-thick diagonal slices. Set aside.

In a 4- to 5-quart pan, combine broth, lemon peel, tarragon, and white pepper; bring to a boil over high heat. Add capellini; when broth returns to a boil, reduce heat and boil gently for 4 minutes. Add shrimp and asparagus. Continue to cook just until shrimp are opaque in center; cut to test (about 3 minutes). Stir in watercress, then lemon juice. Serve immediately (greens will lose their bright color as soup stands). Makes 4 to 6 servings.

Per serving: 135 calories (22% fat, 28% carbohydrates, 50% protein), 3 g total fat (0.8 g saturated fat), 9 g carbohydrates, 17 g protein, 84 mg cholesterol, 165 mg sodium

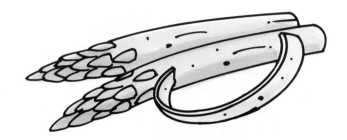

Fish & Pea Soup

Preparation time: About 15 minutes

Cooking time: About 20 minutes

Ladle chunks of lean white fish and tarragon-scented broth into wide bowls, then slice a crusty baguette—and you have a speedy, satisfying family supper.

3	large leeks (about 1¾ lbs. *total*)
2	tablespoons salad oil
1	clove garlic, minced or pressed
1	large carrot (about 4 oz.), finely chopped
1	cup dry white wine or low-sodium chicken broth
6	cups low-sodium chicken broth
1	bay leaf
1	teaspoon dry tarragon
1½	to 2 pounds skinless rockfish or lingcod fillets
1	package (about 10 oz.) frozen tiny peas, broken apart
	Salt and pepper

Cut off and discard root ends and dark green tops of leeks; discard coarse outer leaves. Split leeks lengthwise and rinse well; thinly slice crosswise.

Heat oil in a 5- to 6-quart pan over medium heat. Add leeks, garlic, and carrot; cook, stirring occasionally, until leeks are soft but not browned (6 to 8 minutes). Add wine, broth, bay leaf, and tarragon. Bring to a boil; then reduce heat to medium-low and cook for 5 minutes.

Meanwhile, rinse fish, pat dry, and cut into 1-inch chunks. To pan, add fish and peas. Cover and cook until fish is just opaque but still moist in thickest part; cut to test (about 6 minutes). Season to taste with salt and pepper. Makes 6 servings.

Per serving: 272 calories (29% fat, 26% carbohydrates, 45% protein), 9 g total fat (1 g saturated fat), 18 g carbohydrates, 30 g protein, 46 mg cholesterol, 219 mg sodium

■ *Pictured on page 22*

Harvest Turkey Soup

Preparation time: About 20 minutes

Cooking time: About 40 minutes

Hearty and warming, this meaty soup holds pasta, fragrant herbs, and plenty of fresh vegetables.

Vegetable oil cooking spray

- 1 **pound lean ground turkey**
- 1 **medium-size onion, chopped**
- 1 **teaspoon dry oregano**
- 1 **teaspoon Italian herb seasoning or ¼ teaspoon *each* dry basil, dry marjoram, dry oregano, and dry thyme**
- 3 **large firm-ripe tomatoes (about 1¼ lbs. *total*), chopped**
- 3 **large carrots (about 12 oz. *total*), thinly sliced**
- 1 **large potato (about 8 oz.), peeled and diced**
- 6 **cups beef broth**
- 1 **cup *each* tomato juice and dry red wine**
- 1 **tablespoon Worcestershire**
- ½ **cup small dry pasta shapes, such as tripolini**
- 2 **medium-size zucchini, coarsely diced (about 2 cups)**

About 1 teaspoon liquid hot pepper seasoning

Spray a wide 4- to 5-quart pan with cooking spray. Crumble turkey into pan; add onion, oregano, and herb seasoning. Cook over medium heat, stirring often, until turkey is no longer pink and onion is soft but not browned (about 5 minutes). Stir in tomatoes, carrots, potato, broth, tomato juice, wine, and Worcestershire. Increase heat to medium-high and bring to a boil; reduce heat, cover, and boil gently for 20 minutes. Add pasta, cover, and cook for 5 minutes. Add zucchini and boil gently, uncovered, until pasta is tender to bite (8 to 10 minutes). Add hot pepper seasoning. Makes 6 to 8 servings.

Per serving: 210 calories (26% fat, 42% carbohydrates, 32% protein), 6 g total fat (2 g saturated fat), 22 g carbohydrates, 17 g protein, 47 mg cholesterol, 929 mg sodium

Citrus Chicken Soup

Preparation time: About 25 minutes

Cooking time: About 1 hour

This vibrant chicken soup goes together easily. To make it, you'll need mild fresh chiles; use either the Anaheim (California) or New Mexico variety.

- 4 **chicken breast halves (about 2 lbs. *total*)**
- 6 **cups low-sodium chicken broth**
- 1 **medium-size onion, finely chopped**
- 1 **can (about 14½ oz.) diced tomatoes**
- ½ **teaspoon dry oregano**
- 1 **teaspoon grated lemon peel**
- ¼ **teaspoon pepper**
- 2 **medium-size thin-skinned potatoes (about 10 oz. *total*), scrubbed and diced**
- 1 **medium-size ear corn**
- ⅓ **cup coarsely chopped cilantro**
- 2 **medium-size fresh mild red or green chiles, seeded and finely chopped**
- 1 **small firm-ripe avocado**
- 2 **tablespoons lime juice**

Lime wedges

Rinse chicken, pat dry, and place in a 5- to 6-quart pan. Add broth, onion, tomatoes and their liquid, oregano, lemon peel, and pepper; bring to a boil over medium-high heat. Then reduce heat, cover, and simmer until meat in thickest part is no longer pink; cut to test (about 25 minutes). Lift out chicken and set aside until cool enough to touch.

While chicken is cooling, add potatoes to pan; cover and cook over medium-low heat until potatoes are tender to bite (25 to 30 minutes). Meanwhile, remove and discard skin and bones from chicken; tear meat into bite-size pieces and set aside. Discard husk and silk from corn; cut corn kernels from cob.

Skim and discard fat from soup. Add chicken, corn, cilantro, and chiles. Cook just until heated through (3 to 5 minutes). Meanwhile, pit, peel, and dice avocado; mix gently with lime juice. Offer avocado to sprinkle into soup and lime wedges to squeeze into each serving to taste. Makes 6 servings.

Per serving: 242 calories (26% fat, 29% carbohydrates, 46% protein), 7 g total fat (1 g saturated fat), 17 g carbohydrates, 28 g protein, 57 mg cholesterol, 238 mg sodium

A distinctive blend of Dijon mustard, tart-sweet balsamic vinegar, nippy mustard seeds, and olive oil dresses crisp Watercress, Butter Lettuce & Shrimp Salad (recipe on page 32). Homemade sourdough croutons provide a crunchy accent.

Salads

Salads are high on everyone's list of lowfat dishes. But while it's true that typical salad ingredients such as fruits, greens, and other vegetables are generally low in fat, many of the dressings with which we customarily anoint them aren't. To keep the fat calories in salads to a minimum, the dressings must be streamlined, too—by reducing or omitting some of the oil. Such alterations can throw a dressing's taste off balance, though, since oil is the element that smooths and distributes the other flavors. To prevent this problem, you may wish to choose one of the less sharp vinegars, such as an elegant wine vinegar, rice vinegar, or tart-sweet, barrel-aged balsamic vinegar. You can also replace the vinegar with more subtly flavored lime, lemon, or orange juice.

Any oil you do use in a salad dressing should be a heart-healthy choice. Distinctive-tasting olive oil is high in monounsaturated fat; polyunsaturated oils such as corn, safflower, and sunflower are more neutral in flavor than olive oil, as are canola and avocado oils (both high in monounsaturated fat).

Produce makes up the bulk of the salad, so it's important to select the very freshest offerings from market or garden. And to conserve nutrients, crispness, bright color, and flavor, prepare and cut your fruits and vegetables just before you serve the salad.

■ Pictured on page 30

Watercress, Butter Lettuce & Shrimp Salad

Preparation time: About 10 minutes, plus at least 10 minutes to soak mustard seeds

Baking time: 12 to 15 minutes

Oven-browned croutons provide a crisp accent for a pert first-course salad lightly dressed with balsamic vinegar, Dijon mustard, and whole mustard seeds.

> 1 tablespoon mustard seeds
>
> ¼ cup boiling water
>
> Olive oil cooking spray
>
> 2 cups ½-inch cubes sourdough French bread
>
> ¼ cup balsamic or red wine vinegar
>
> 2 teaspoons Dijon mustard
>
> 1 tablespoon olive oil or salad oil
>
> 2 quarts torn butter lettuce leaves, rinsed and crisped
>
> 3 cups lightly packed watercress sprigs, rinsed and crisped
>
> 8 ounces small cooked shrimp

Place mustard seeds in a small bowl; pour boiling water over them. Let stand for at least 10 minutes or up to 8 hours; drain well.

Spray a shallow rimmed baking pan with cooking spray. Spread bread cubes in pan; spray with cooking spray. Bake in a 350° oven until crisp and golden brown (12 to 15 minutes). Let cool in pan on a rack. If made ahead, store airtight at room temperature for up to 2 days.

In a small bowl, stir together mustard seeds, vinegar, mustard, and oil. Arrange lettuce, watercress, and shrimp in a large salad bowl; add mustard seed dressing and mix lightly until greens are coated. Top with croutons. Makes 6 servings.

Per serving: 123 calories (29% fat, 35% carbohydrates, 36% protein), 4 g total fat (1 g saturated fat), 11 g carbohydrates, 11 g protein, 74 mg cholesterol, 228 mg sodium

■ Pictured on page 11

Orange & Olive Patio Salad

Preparation time: About 20 minutes, plus about 1 hour to cool dressing

Cooking time: About 1 minute

A salad is the quintessential "light" dish—but even so, it's surprising how quickly the calories can add up. By using water in place of oil in the dressing, we've cut this refreshing salad's fat calories to a minimum.

> ½ cup water
>
> 1 teaspoon arrowroot
>
> 4 teaspoons honey
>
> 2 tablespoons finely chopped fresh mint
>
> 1 small mild red onion, thinly sliced crosswise
>
> ¼ cup wine vinegar
>
> 6 cups mixed torn butter lettuce and radicchio leaves (or all butter lettuce leaves), rinsed and crisped
>
> 6 cups lightly packed watercress sprigs, rinsed and crisped
>
> 2 medium-size oranges (about 1 lb. *total*), peeled and thinly sliced crosswise
>
> ¼ cup small pitted ripe or Niçoise olives
>
> ¼ cup lime juice
>
> About ¼ cup mixed fresh basil and fresh mint leaves (optional)
>
> Salt and pepper

In a small pan, combine water, arrowroot, honey, and chopped mint. Bring to a boil over high heat, stirring constantly. Remove from heat and let stand until cold (about 1 hour).

Meanwhile, in a large salad bowl, combine onion and vinegar. Let stand for at least 15 minutes or up to 3 hours. Drain, discarding vinegar; separate onion slices into rings. In same salad bowl, combine onion rings, lettuce, radicchio, and watercress; mix lightly. Top with orange slices and olives. Stir lime juice into honey-mint mixture, then pour through a fine wire strainer onto salad; discard residue. Garnish with basil and mint leaves, if desired; season to taste with salt and pepper. Makes 8 to 10 servings.

Per serving: 43 calories (11% fat, 78% carbohydrates, 11% protein), 0.6 g total fat (0.1 g saturated fat), 9 g carbohydrates, 1 g protein, 0 mg cholesterol, 46 mg sodium

Wilted Spinach Salad with Oranges

Preparation time: About 15 minutes

Cooking time: 6 to 8 minutes

A little heat can heighten flavors. Here, onion rings warmed in a blend of balsamic vinegar, tarragon, and fresh orange peel enliven a green-and-gold combination of spinach and orange segments.

- 2   **medium-size oranges (about 1 lb. *total*)**
- 2   **quarts lightly packed spinach leaves, rinsed and crisped**
- 1   **large onion, thinly sliced and separated into rings**
- ¼   **cup balsamic or red wine vinegar**
- 2   **teaspoons salad oil**
- 1   **teaspoon dry tarragon**

Grate 1 teaspoon peel (colored part only) from one of the oranges; set aside. With a sharp knife, cut remaining peel and all white membrane from both oranges. Holding fruit over a bowl to catch juice, cut between membranes to free segments; place segments in bowl with juice and set aside. Place spinach in a large salad bowl.

In a wide frying pan, combine onion, vinegar, oil, tarragon, and grated orange peel. Place over medium-low heat, cover, and cook until onions are tender-crisp when pierced (6 to 8 minutes). Gently stir in orange segments and juice. Pour orange mixture over spinach. Mix lightly, then serve at once. Makes 4 servings.

Per serving: 86 calories (26% fat, 63% carbohydrates, 11% protein), 3 g total fat (0.3 g saturated fat), 15 g carbohydrates, 3 g protein, 0 mg cholesterol, 35 mg sodium

Watercress & Pear Salad

Preparation time: About 10 minutes, plus about 30 minutes to cool figs

Cooking time: 35 to 40 minutes

Ingredients chosen for their contrasting textures and flavors distinguish this attractive first-course salad. A base of peppery watercress is topped with buttery pears, tender dried figs, and a sweet-hot crystallized ginger dressing.

- 3   **tablespoons chopped crystallized ginger**
- 6   **dried figs (about 4 oz. *total*)**
- ½   **cup sherry vinegar or seasoned rice vinegar (or use ½ cup white wine vinegar plus 4 teaspoons sugar)**
-     **About ¾ cup water**
- 2   **tablespoons olive oil or salad oil**
- 2   **large firm-ripe Comice or Anjou pears (about 1¼ lbs. *total*)**
- 4   **cups lightly packed watercress sprigs, rinsed and crisped**

In a small pan, combine ginger, figs, vinegar, and ½ cup of the water. Bring to a boil over high heat; reduce heat, cover, and simmer until figs are very tender when pierced (35 to 40 minutes). Set pan aside and let stand, covered, until figs are completely cool (about 30 minutes).

Drain fig cooking liquid into a glass measure; if necessary, add enough water to make ⅔ cup. Set aside the 3 best-looking figs. Place remaining 3 figs, cooking liquid, and oil in a blender or food processor; whirl until smooth. (At this point, you may cover and refrigerate figs and dressing separately for up to a day.)

Just before serving, peel and core pears; cut lengthwise into ¼-inch slices. Divide watercress equally among 6 salad plates. Fan a sixth of the pear slices over watercress on each plate. Cut reserved 3 figs into halves; place a fig half at base of each pear fan. Spoon dressing over pears. Makes 6 servings.

Per serving: 172 calories (25% fat, 72% carbohydrates, 3% protein), 5 g total fat (0.7 g saturated fat), 33 g carbohydrates, 1 g protein, 0 mg cholesterol, 20 mg sodium

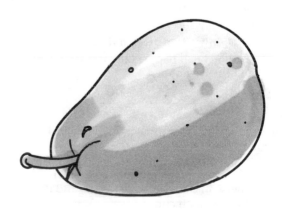

■ *Pictured on facing page*

Black Bean, Corn & Pepper Salad

Preparation time: About 15 minutes

Chilling time: At least 1 hour

This substantial salad nicely complements favorite outdoor fare. Try it with grilled beef or alongside a barbecued, lime- and chile-rubbed turkey breast.

   2   cans (about 15 oz. *each)* black beans or cannellini (white kidney beans), drained and rinsed

   1½   cups cooked fresh corn kernels or 1 package (10 oz.) frozen corn kernels, thawed

   1   large red bell pepper (about 8 oz.), seeded and finely chopped

   2   small fresh jalapeño chiles, seeded and finely chopped

   ½   cup firmly packed chopped cilantro

   ¼   cup lime juice

   2   tablespoons salad oil

      Salt and pepper

      Lettuce leaves, rinsed and crisped

      Lime wedges and cilantro sprigs (optional)

In a large bowl, combine beans, corn, bell pepper, chiles, chopped cilantro, lime juice, and oil; mix lightly. Season to taste with salt and pepper. Cover and refrigerate for at least 1 hour or up to a day.

To serve, line a serving bowl with lettuce leaves; spoon in bean mixture. (Or spoon bean mixture into lettuce cups on individual plates.) Garnish with lime wedges and cilantro sprigs, if desired. Makes 6 servings.

Per serving: 193 calories (26% fat, 56% carbohydrates, 18% protein), 6 g total fat (0.7 g saturated fat), 28 g carbohydrates, 9 g protein, 0 mg cholesterol, 186 mg sodium

Potato Salad with Seed Vinaigrette

Preparation time: About 15 minutes

Cooking time: 30 to 35 minutes

A light vinaigrette, fragrant with herb seeds, seasons this picnic-perfect potato salad. (This is one potato salad you can safely serve at room temperature.)

      Seed Vinaigrette (recipe follows)

   5   large red thin-skinned potatoes (2 to 2½ lbs. *total),* scrubbed

   1   cup thinly sliced celery

   ½   cup thinly sliced green onions

   1   small red bell pepper (about 5 oz.), seeded and finely chopped

      Salt

Prepare Seed Vinaigrette and set aside.

Place unpeeled potatoes in a 5- to 6-quart pan and add enough water to cover. Bring to a boil over high heat. Reduce heat, partially cover, and boil gently until potatoes are tender when pierced (25 to 30 minutes). Drain, immerse in cold water until cool, and drain again. Cut into ¾-inch cubes.

In a large bowl, gently mix potatoes, celery, onions, bell pepper, and Seed Vinaigrette. Season to taste with salt. If made ahead, cover and refrigerate for up to a day. Serve cold or at room temperature. Makes 6 to 8 servings.

■ **Seed Vinaigrette.** In a wide frying pan, combine 1 teaspoon *each* **mustard seeds, cumin seeds,** and **fennel seeds.** Cook over medium heat until fragrant (3 to 5 minutes), shaking pan often. Using back of a heavy spoon, coarsely crush seeds. Remove from heat and mix in 2 tablespoons **salad oil,** ⅓ cup **cider vinegar,** ½ teaspoon **coarsely ground pepper,** and 1 clove **garlic** (minced or pressed).

Per serving: 155 calories (25% fat, 67% carbohydrates, 8% protein), 4 g total fat (0.5 g saturated fat), 27 g carbohydrates, 3 g protein, 0 mg cholesterol, 27 mg sodium

*Smoky barbecued turkey breast, colorful Black Bean, Corn
& Pepper Salad (recipe on facing page), and a basket of freshly
baked Southwest Blue Cornbread Sticks (recipe on page 85)
add up to a memorable Santa Fe–style meal.*

Lowfat Dressings

A good dressing doesn't just sink to the bottom of the bowl—it coats all the salad ingredients. Though this clinging quality is usually provided by oil, leaner choices can be just as effective. We suggest you thicken your dressings with arrowroot (or other cooked starch) or with purées of fruit or chiles.

Strawberry-Tarragon Dressing

Preparation time: About 15 minutes
Cooking time: About 3 minutes

1½ cups strawberries, hulled
    About ¼ cup lemon juice
1 tablespoon sugar
1 tablespoon finely chopped shallot
1 teaspoon chopped fresh tarragon or ½ teaspoon dry tarragon
½ teaspoon cornstarch
2 tablespoons orange juice

Whirl strawberries in a blender or food processor until puréed. Rub through a fine wire strainer into a 2-cup glass measure. Add ¼ cup of the lemon juice and enough water to make 1 cup. Transfer to a small pan and add sugar, shallot, and tarragon.

Smoothly mix cornstarch and orange juice; stir into strawberry mixture. Bring to a boil over high heat, stirring constantly. Set pan in a bowl of ice water to chill mixture quickly; then taste and add more lemon juice, if needed. If made ahead, cover and refrigerate for up to a day. Makes about 1 cup.

Per tablespoon: 10 calories (5% fat, 90% carbohydrates, 5% protein), 0.1 g total fat (0 g saturated fat), 2 g carbohydrates, 0.1 g protein, 0 mg cholesterol, 1 mg sodium

Garlic Buttermilk Dressing

Preparation time: About 5 minutes

½ cup lowfat buttermilk
1 tablespoon seasoned rice vinegar (or 1 tablespoon white wine vinegar plus ½ teaspoon sugar)
2 teaspoons Dijon mustard
¼ teaspoon *each* salt and pepper
3 green onions, thinly sliced
1 clove garlic, minced or pressed

In a small bowl, stir together buttermilk, vinegar, mustard, salt, pepper, onions, and garlic. If made ahead, cover and refrigerate for up to a day. Makes about ⅔ cup.

Per tablespoon: 9 calories (17% fat, 61% carbohydrates, 22% protein), 0.2 g total fat (0.1 g saturated fat), 1 g carbohydrates, 0.5 g protein, 0.5 mg cholesterol, 97 mg sodium

Shallot Dressing

Preparation time: About 5 minutes
Cooking time: About 2 minutes

⅔ cup water
1 teaspoon arrowroot
1 tablespoon Dijon mustard
¼ cup finely slivered shallots
¼ cup sherry vinegar

In a small pan, blend water and arrowroot. Bring to a boil over high heat, stirring constantly. Set pan in a bowl of ice water to chill mixture quickly; then stir in mustard, shallots, and vinegar. If made ahead, cover and refrigerate for up to a day. Makes about 1 cup.

Per tablespoon: 4 calories (12% fat, 82% carbohydrates, 6% protein), 0.1 g total fat (0 g saturated fat), 0.9 g carbohydrates, 0.1 g protein, 0 mg cholesterol, 28 mg sodium

Green Chile Dressing

Preparation time: About 10 minutes

1 small can (about 4 oz.) green chiles
⅓ cup lime juice
¼ cup *each* water and chopped cilantro
1 clove garlic
1 or 2 small fresh jalapeño chiles, seeded and chopped
1½ teaspoons sugar
    Salt

In a blender or food processor, combine green chiles, lime juice, water, cilantro, garlic, jalapeño chiles, and sugar; whirl until puréed. Season to taste with salt. If made ahead, cover and refrigerate for up to a day. Makes about 1 cup.

Per tablespoon: 5 calories (2% fat, 92% carbohydrates, 7% protein), 0.1 g total fat (0 g saturated fat), 1 g carbohydrates, 0.1 g protein, 0 mg cholesterol, 44 mg sodium

Lemon Shrimp Seviche Salad

Preparation time: *About 30 minutes*

Cooking time: *About 8 minutes*

Chilling time: *At least 1½ hours*

In a classic seviche, the seafood is "cooked" without heat in lime or lemon juice—but in this light main-dish salad, the shrimp are actually lightly poached, acquiring favorite seviche flavors in the process.

- ¾ cup *each* lemon juice and cider vinegar
- 1 tablespoon drained capers
- 1 teaspoon Dijon mustard
- 1 pound medium-large raw shrimp (36 to 42 per lb.), shelled and deveined
- 4 green onions, thinly sliced
- 2 medium-size pear-shaped (Roma-type) tomatoes (about 4 oz. *total*), finely chopped
- 1 small yellow bell pepper (about 5 oz.), seeded and thinly sliced

Lemon wedges
Salt and pepper

In a wide frying pan, combine lemon juice, vinegar, capers, and mustard. Bring to a boil over high heat. Add shrimp, reduce heat to low, cover, and simmer just until opaque in center; cut to test (3 to 4 minutes). Using a slotted spoon, transfer shrimp to a bowl. Increase heat to high and boil liquid until reduced to 1 cup (about 4 minutes). Pour liquid over shrimp; let cool, then cover and refrigerate until cold (at least 1½ hours) or for up to 8 hours.

To shrimp, add onions, tomatoes, and bell pepper; mix lightly. Spoon into 4 shallow bowls; spoon liquid over mixture. Garnish with lemon wedges and season to taste with salt and pepper. Makes 4 servings.

Per serving: 131 calories (13% fat, 30% carbohydrates, 57% protein), 2 g total fat (0.3 g saturated fat), 10 g carbohydrates, 20 g protein, 140 mg cholesterol, 242 mg sodium

■ *Pictured on page 3*

Chinese Noodle Salad with Five-spice Chicken

Preparation time: *About 15 minutes*

Cooking time: *8 to 11 minutes*

Asian flavors star in this entrée. Served on a bed of spinach, both the cool pasta and hot chicken are seasoned with soy, sesame oil, and fragrant five-spice.

Five-spice Dressing (recipe follows)
- 10 ounces (about 3 cups; part of a 14-oz. package) fresh Chinese-style noodles
- ½ cup coarsely chopped cilantro
- 1 tablespoon grated fresh ginger
- ½ teaspoon grated lemon peel
- 4 chicken breast halves (about 2 lbs. *total*), skinned and boned
- 4 to 6 cups spinach leaves, rinsed and crisped
- ¼ cup thinly sliced green onions

Prepare Five-spice Dressing and set aside.

In a 5- to 6-quart pan, bring 3 quarts water to a boil over high heat, then add noodles and cook just until tender to bite (2 to 3 minutes). Drain, immerse in cold water until cool, and drain again. Transfer to a large bowl. Add ¼ cup of the dressing; then add cilantro, ginger, and lemon peel. Mix gently and set aside.

Rinse chicken; pat dry. Place on a lightly greased grill 4 to 6 inches above a solid bed of medium-hot coals. Cook, turning once and basting with some of the remaining dressing, until meat in thickest part is no longer pink; cut to test (6 to 8 minutes). Place chicken on a board; cut into ½-inch-wide slices.

Line 4 dinner plates with spinach. Top with noodles and chicken; drizzle with any remaining dressing, then sprinkle with onions. Makes 4 servings.

■ *Five-spice Dressing.* Mix 2 tablespoons **seasoned rice vinegar** (or 2 tablespoons white wine vinegar plus 1 teaspoon sugar), 1 tablespoon *each* **soy sauce** and **lemon juice**, 1 clove **garlic** (minced or pressed), ½ teaspoon **Chinese five-spice powder** (or ⅛ teaspoon *each* ground cloves, crushed anise seeds, ground cinnamon, and ground ginger), 1 tablespoon **Oriental sesame oil**, and 2 tablespoons **salad oil**.

Per serving: 487 calories (26% fat, 37% carbohydrates, 37% protein), 14 g total fat (2 g saturated fat), 44 g carbohydrates, 45 g protein, 169 mg cholesterol, 430 mg sodium

*Accompanied with hot corn on the cob and served atop
herb-seasoned pasta, Grilled Beef & Peppers with Orzo (recipe on
page 40) features skewered bell pepper wedges and steak strips flavored
in a red wine marinade. Fresh rosemary sprigs, tucked into the skewers, release
a tempting aroma as the meat sizzles on the barbecue.*

Meats

Being health-conscious doesn't mean shunning all red meats. Beef, lamb, pork, and veal fit right into a lowfat diet: today's meat animals are bred to be lean, and with wise shopping and preparation, you can cut fat still further. At the market, select the leanest cuts you can find; at home, carefully trim away any surface fat. In cooking, use as little fat as possible—and make sure that whatever you do use is unsaturated (see page 101).

In this chapter, you'll learn some of the best ways to prepare lean meat. Grilling and broiling require virtually no fat and work well for tender cuts such as beef top round, loin lamb chops, and pork tenderloin. Braising and stewing—using our lowfat "sweating" technique—produce fork-tender beef, lamb, and veal with the distinctive flavor that develops during long, slow simmering. Hunter's-style Lamb Stew and Oven Beef & Mushroom Stew in Bourbon are two examples of lean yet exceptionally rich-tasting dishes.

Roast lean meats can be superb, too; for a special occasion, try our boneless butterflied leg of lamb with yams and onions.

When you serve meat, limit portion size to a sensible 3 ounces (cooked weight). To round out meals, avoid high-fat foods and stick to lean choices, such as whole-grain breads, fruits, raw or simply cooked vegetables, pasta, and hearty grains like rice, couscous, polenta, and bulgur.

■ *Pictured on page 38*

Grilled Beef & Peppers with Orzo

Preparation time: About 20 minutes, plus at least 30 minutes to marinate meat

Cooking time: About 25 minutes

Here's an appealing dinner from the backyard grill: skewers of multicolored bell peppers and pounded, marinated top round steak. Accompany the meat with rice-shaped pasta dotted with toasted pine nuts.

    1   **tablespoon lemon juice**

    1   **teaspoon olive oil**

  ⅓   **cup dry red wine**

 1½   **pounds boneless beef top round (about ½ inch thick), trimmed of fat**

    1   *each* **small green, red, and yellow bell pepper (about 5 oz.** *each)*

  12   **rosemary sprigs (***each* **about 3 inches long)**

        Herbed Orzo (recipe follows)

        Salt and pepper

Set a large heavy-duty plastic bag in a shallow pan. In bag, combine lemon juice, oil, and wine.

Cut beef across the grain into 6 long strips; place between sheets of plastic wrap, then pound with flat side of a meat mallet until each piece is about ¼ inch thick. Cut each bell pepper lengthwise into sixths; remove and discard seeds. Add beef strips and peppers to marinade in bag; seal bag and turn to coat beef and peppers with marinade. Refrigerate for at least 30 minutes or up to a day.

Lift beef strips and peppers from bag, reserving marinade. On each of 6 metal skewers (at least 10 inches long), weave one beef strip and 3 bell pepper pieces (one of each color), rippling beef slightly around peppers. For each skewer, tuck 2 rosemary sprigs between meat and skewer. Set skewers aside while you prepare Herbed Orzo.

Place skewers on a lightly greased grill 4 to 6 inches above a solid bed of hot coals. Cook, turning as needed and brushing with marinade, until meat is browned on outside and done to your liking; cut to test (6 to 8 minutes for rare). Season to taste with salt and pepper. Serve with Herbed Orzo. Makes 6 servings.

■ *Herbed Orzo.* Toast 2 tablespoons **pine nuts** in a small nonstick frying pan over medium-low heat until lightly browned (about 3 minutes), stirring. Remove from pan and let cool. Heat 1 tablespoon **olive oil** in same pan; add 2 cloves **garlic** (minced or pressed), 1 teaspoon **dry basil,** and ½ teaspoon **dry marjoram.** Cook, stirring, until garlic is soft but not browned (about 2 minutes). Remove from heat and set aside.

In a 3- to 4-quart pan, cook 1 cup (5 to 7 oz.) **orzo** or other dry rice-shaped pasta in 2 quarts boiling water until tender to bite (about 10 minutes); or cook according to package directions. Drain well, transfer to a warm bowl, and mix gently with garlic mixture, pine nuts, and 1 tablespoon **tarragon vinegar.**

Per serving: *304 calories (25% fat, 41% carbohydrates, 34% protein), 9 g total fat (2 g saturated fat), 31 g carbohydrates, 26 g protein, 53 mg cholesterol, 46 mg sodium*

Oven Beef & Mushroom Stew in Bourbon

Preparation time: About 20 minutes

Baking time: About 2 hours and 50 minutes

A generous measure of bourbon whiskey, a touch of Dijon mustard, and four members of the onion family—garlic, red onions, shallots, and chives—give this easy oven-cooked stew its rich flavor and complex aroma. Serve the tender beef and abundant gravy with baked russet or sweet potatoes.

- 2 **pounds boneless beef round tip, trimmed of fat and cut into 1-inch cubes**
- 2 **to 3 tablespoons all-purpose flour**
- ¾ **cup bourbon**
- ¼ **cup soy sauce**
- 1 **cup water**
- 2 **tablespoons** *each* **Dijon mustard and firmly packed brown sugar**
- 1 **clove garlic, minced or pressed**
- 1 **teaspoon Worcestershire sauce**
- 8 **ounces small mushrooms (or large mushrooms, quartered)**
- 2 **small red onions, peeled and quartered lengthwise**
- 4 **ounces shallots, peeled**
  Snipped chives

Coat beef cubes with flour and shake off excess; then arrange cubes slightly apart in an ungreased 9- by 13-inch baking dish or pan. Bake in a 500° oven for 20 minutes. Meanwhile, in a bowl, stir together bourbon, soy sauce, water, mustard, sugar, garlic, and Worcestershire. Set aside.

Remove beef cubes from oven and let cool in baking dish for about 5 minutes. Reduce oven temperature to 350°. Gradually add bourbon mixture to beef in dish, stirring to scrape up browned bits. Then stir in mushrooms, onions, and shallots. Cover tightly and bake until beef is very tender when pierced (about 2½ hours), stirring once or twice. Garnish with chives. Makes 8 servings.

Per serving: 199 calories (22% fat, 25% carbohydrates, 53% protein), 5 g total fat (1 g saturated fat), 12 g carbohydrates, 26 g protein, 68 mg cholesterol, 709 mg sodium

Garlic Pork Chops with Balsamic Vinegar

Preparation time: 15 to 20 minutes

Cooking time: About 20 minutes

Dark, rich-tasting balsamic vinegar is a specialty from the area around Modena, Italy. Combined with an abundance of sweet blanched, sautéed garlic, it makes a tempting sauce for quickly cooked pork chops.

- 1 **head garlic (about 1½ oz.), separated into cloves**
- 6 **center-cut loin pork chops (about 2 lbs.** *total)***, trimmed of fat**
  Freshly ground pepper
  Vegetable oil cooking spray
- 1 **package (about 12 oz.) eggless noodles**
- ¼ **cup sweet vermouth**
- 1 **tablespoon Dijon mustard**
- ⅓ **cup balsamic vinegar**
  Salt

In a medium-size pan, bring about 4 cups water to a boil. Add unpeeled garlic cloves; boil for 1 minute. Drain; let cool slightly, then peel and set aside.

Sprinkle chops generously with pepper. Spray a wide frying pan with cooking spray and place over medium-high heat. Add chops and cook until well browned on bottom (4 to 5 minutes). Turn chops over, arrange garlic around them, and continue to cook until browned on other side (4 to 5 more minutes).

Meanwhile, in a 6-quart pan, cook noodles in 3 quarts boiling water just until tender to bite (10 to 12 minutes); or cook according to package directions.

While noodles are cooking, mix vermouth and mustard; pour over browned chops. Reduce heat to low, cover, and cook until chops are done but still moist and slightly pink in center; cut to test (about 5 minutes). Drain noodles; transfer to a warm deep platter. Arrange chops over noodles; keep warm.

Add vinegar to sauce in pan. Increase heat to medium-high and stir to scrape up browned bits. Bring to a boil; boil until reduced to about ½ cup (2 to 3 minutes). Season sauce to taste with salt, then spoon over chops. Makes 6 servings.

Per serving: 387 calories (18% fat, 49% carbohydrates, 33% protein), 8 g total fat (3 g saturated fat), 47 g carbohydrates, 31 g protein, 64 mg cholesterol, 168 mg sodium

Grilled Pork with Couscous

Preparation time: About 30 minutes, plus at least 30 minutes to marinate meat

Cooking time: About 30 minutes

For a tempting summer barbecue meal, serve grilled pork tenderloin with crisp snow peas and gingery couscous.

> 2 **pork tenderloins (1½ to 2 lbs. *total*)**
> ¼ **cup soy sauce**
> 2 **tablespoons sake or dry sherry**
> 1½ **tablespoons honey**
> 1 **tablespoon grated fresh ginger**
> 1 **clove garlic, minced or pressed**
> 1 **pound Chinese pea pods (also called snow peas), ends and strings removed**
> **Golden Curried Couscous (page 80)**

Trim fat and silvery membranes from pork tenderloins. Fold thin end of each tenderloin under to make meat evenly thick; tie to secure. Set a heavy-duty plastic bag in a shallow pan. In bag, combine soy sauce, sake, honey, ginger, and garlic. Add pork; seal bag and turn to coat pork with marinade. Refrigerate for at least 30 minutes or up to a day.

Bring 3 quarts water to a boil in a 5- to 6-quart pan over high heat. Add pea pods; cook just until they turn a brighter green (about 2 minutes). Drain, immerse in cold water until cool, and drain again. Set aside.

Lift pork from bag, reserving marinade. Place pork on a lightly greased grill 4 to 6 inches above a solid bed of medium coals. Cook, turning to brown evenly and brushing often with marinade, just until pork is no longer pink in thickest part; cut to test (20 to 25 minutes). Meanwhile, prepare Golden Curried Couscous.

To serve, thinly slice pork and arrange in center of a platter; surround with pea pods and couscous. Makes 6 servings.

Per serving with Golden Curried Couscous: 553 calories (17% fat, 53% carbohydrates, 30% protein), 11 g total fat (3 g saturated fat), 73 g carbohydrates, 42 g protein, 97 mg cholesterol, 826 mg sodium

■ *Pictured on facing page*

Baked Polenta with Veal Sauce

Preparation time: About 15 minutes

Cooking time: 40 to 45 minutes

Soft, creamy baked polenta is delicious on its own as a side dish—but even better when topped with a lean, herb-seasoned veal and tomato sauce.

> **Baked Polenta (recipe follows)**
> 1 **teaspoon olive oil**
> 1 **small onion, finely chopped**
> 1 **small carrot (about 2 oz.), shredded**
> 4 **ounces mushrooms, quartered**
> 1 **clove garlic, minced or pressed**
> 2 **teaspoons Italian herb seasoning or ½ teaspoon *each* dry basil, dry marjoram, dry oregano, and dry thyme**
> 1 **pound lean ground veal**
> 1 **large can (about 28 oz.) pear-shaped tomatoes**
> ¼ **cup tomato paste**
> ½ **cup dry white wine**
> **Grated Parmesan cheese (optional)**

Prepare Baked Polenta. While polenta is baking, heat oil in a wide nonstick frying pan over medium-high heat. Add onion, carrot, mushrooms, garlic, and herb seasoning. Cook, stirring often, until onion is soft (about 5 minutes). Crumble veal into pan; cook, stirring often, until it begins to brown. Cut up tomatoes; then add tomatoes and their liquid, tomato paste, and wine to pan. Bring to a boil. Adjust heat so sauce boils gently; cook, stirring occasionally, until thickened (about 20 minutes).

Spoon Baked Polenta into wide, shallow bowls and top with veal sauce. Offer cheese to add to taste, if desired. Makes 4 to 6 servings.

■ *Baked Polenta.* In a greased shallow 2-quart baking dish, mix 4 cups **low-sodium chicken broth,** 1¼ cups **polenta** (Italian-style cornmeal), ¼ cup finely chopped **onion,** and 1 tablespoon **olive oil.** Bake in a 350° oven until liquid has been absorbed (40 to 45 minutes).

Per serving: 376 calories (29% fat, 44% carbohydrates, 27% protein), 12 g total fat (3 g saturated fat), 42 g carbohydrates, 25 g protein, 74 mg cholesterol, 494 mg sodium

No more stirring! When you make Baked Polenta with Veal Sauce (recipe on facing page), you needn't stand guard over a simmering pot—the creamy Italian-style cornmeal mush cooks unattended in the oven, leaving you free to assemble the richly flavored tomato-mushroom sauce. Complete a hearty supper with crusty rolls and red wine.

Minted Lamb Chops & Mushrooms with Pilaf

Preparation time: About 15 minutes, plus at least 30 minutes to marinate meat

Cooking time: 50 to 55 minutes

If you're planning a patio party, here's the perfect entrée: juicy grilled lamb chops, skewered mushrooms, and an unusual rice and tomato salad.

Pilaf Salad (recipe follows)

4 **loin lamb chops,** *each* **about 1 inch thick (about 1½ lbs.** *total),* **trimmed of fat**

1 **teaspoon olive oil**

2 **tablespoons dry vermouth**

½ **teaspoon pepper**

¼ **cup coarsely chopped fresh mint**

16 **medium-large mushrooms (1 lb.** *total)*

Cherry tomatoes and mint sprigs

Prepare Pilaf Salad. While salad is chilling, set a large heavy-duty plastic bag in a bowl. Place chops in bag; add oil, vermouth, pepper, and chopped mint. Seal bag; turn to coat chops with marinade. Refrigerate for at least 30 minutes or up to a day.

Thread mushrooms onto 4 slender metal skewers. Lift chops from bag, reserving marinade. Brush mushrooms with marinade. Place chops on a lightly greased grill 4 to 6 inches above a solid bed of hot coals; place skewered mushrooms at edges of grill, where heat is less intense. Cook, turning chops once and mushrooms several times, until mushrooms are lightly browned and chops are browned on outside but still pink in center; cut to test (about 10 minutes).

Spoon Pilaf Salad onto a platter; arrange chops and skewered mushrooms over salad. Garnish with cherry tomatoes and mint sprigs. Makes 4 servings.

■ *Pilaf Salad.* Rinse and drain ½ cup **wild rice;** place in a 2- to 3-quart pan and add 1¾ cups **low-sodium chicken broth** and 1 cup **water.** Bring to a boil over high heat; then reduce heat, cover, and simmer for 20 minutes. To partially cooked wild rice, add ¾ cup **long-grain brown rice.** Continue to cook, covered, until all rice is tender to bite (20 to 25 more minutes). Remove from heat. With a fork, stir in 3 tablespoons **lemon juice** and ¼ cup **sliced ripe olives.** Cover and refrigerate until cool (about 30 minutes) or for up to a day. Stir in ⅓ cup **plain lowfat yogurt** and 1 cup halved **cherry tomatoes;** season to taste with **salt.**

Per serving: 431 calories (23% fat, 49% carbohydrates, 28% protein), 11 g total fat (3 g saturated fat), 53 g carbohydrates, 30 g protein, 64 mg cholesterol, 180 mg sodium

Hunter's-style Lamb Stew

Preparation time: About 25 minutes

Cooking time: About 1½ hours

Served with garlicky roasted potatoes, this meaty lamb-mushroom stew is bound to win compliments.

2 **pounds boneless loin or leg of lamb, trimmed of fat and cut into 1-inch chunks**

2 **teaspoons olive oil**

1½ **cups dry white wine**

8 **ounces mushrooms, quartered**

2 **cloves garlic, minced or pressed**

2 **tablespoons fresh or dry rosemary**

Garlic Potatoes (page 76)

¾ **teaspoon cornstarch**

1 **tablespoon cold water**

2 **tablespoons red wine vinegar**

Salt and pepper

In a wide 3½- to 4-quart pan, combine lamb, oil, and ½ cup of the wine. Place over medium heat, cover, and cook gently for 30 minutes. Add mushrooms, garlic, and rosemary; cook, uncovered, stirring occasionally, until almost all liquid has evaporated and juices are browned (25 to 30 minutes). Meanwhile, prepare Garlic Potatoes.

Add remaining 1 cup wine to pan, stirring to scrape up browned bits. Reduce heat, cover, and continue to simmer until lamb is very tender when pierced (25 to 30 more minutes). Blend cornstarch and water, pour into pan, and cook, stirring, until liquid is bubbly. Stir in vinegar, then season to taste with salt and pepper. Serve with Garlic Potatoes. Makes 8 servings.

Per serving with Garlic Potatoes: 317 calories (25% fat, 40% carbohydrates, 35% protein), 9 g total fat (3 g saturated fat), 32 g carbohydrates, 28 g protein, 75 mg cholesterol, 93 mg sodium

Gingered Butterflied Lamb with Yams

Preparation time: About 25 minutes, plus at least 4 hours to marinate meat

Roasting time: About 1 hour

A tart and spicy marinade flavors every part of this entrée—oven-roasted yam wedges, tender onion halves, and thinly sliced boned leg of lamb.

⅓	**cup chopped fresh ginger**
8	**cloves garlic**
¼	**teaspoon pepper**
1½	**tablespoons soy sauce**
¾	**cup red wine vinegar**
2	**to 2½ pounds boneless butterflied leg of lamb**
2	**teaspoons sugar**
¼	**cup raisins**
	Vegetable oil cooking spray
8	**to 10 small yams or sweet potatoes (3½ to 4 lbs. *total*), scrubbed**
8	**to 10 small onions (*each* about 2 inches in diameter), unpeeled, cut into halves lengthwise**
1	**cup beef broth**

In a food processor or blender, combine ginger, garlic, pepper, soy sauce, and 2 tablespoons of the vinegar. Whirl until mixture forms a paste; set aside.

Trim and discard surface fat from lamb. Lay lamb flat in a 9- by 13-inch baking dish; spoon ginger mixture around lamb. Mix sugar, raisins, and remaining 10 tablespoons vinegar; pour over lamb. Cover and refrigerate for at least 4 hours or up to a day.

Spray a roasting pan (12 by 17 inches or larger) with cooking spray. Cut unpeeled yams lengthwise into ¾-inch-thick wedges. Arrange yams and onion halves (cut sides down) in pan. Spray all vegetables

with cooking spray. Roast on lower rack of a 425° oven for 15 minutes.

Meanwhile, lift lamb from dish, reserving marinade. Place lamb, boned side down, on a rack in a shallow baking pan. Insert a meat thermometer in thickest part.

After vegetables have roasted for 15 minutes, place lamb in oven on middle rack. Continue to roast both lamb and vegetables, basting lamb occasionally with marinade, for 30 minutes. Lift raisins from marinade and sprinkle over lamb. Drizzle vegetables with all but 3 tablespoons of the remaining marinade. Continue to roast until vegetables are tender when pierced and thermometer registers 140° to 145°F for medium-rare (10 to 15 more minutes).

Transfer lamb, onions, and yams to a platter; cover lightly with foil and keep warm. To lamb cooking pan, add broth and reserved 3 tablespoons marinade; cook over medium heat, stirring to scrape up browned bits, until reduced to about ¾ cup.

Cut lamb across the grain into thin slices; serve with onions, yams, and sauce to add to taste. Makes 8 to 10 servings.

Per serving: 322 calories (16% fat, 51% carbohydrates, 33% protein), 6 g total fat (2 g saturated fat), 40 g carbohydrates, 26 g protein, 73 mg cholesterol, 353 mg sodium

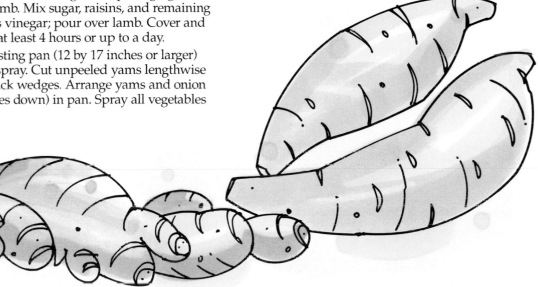

Lean egg whites and a blend of diced chicken thighs seasoned
with onion, parsley, and pungent fennel seeds make a savory, glistening
sauce for tender pasta strands. Serve satisfying Chicken Vermicelli
Carbonara (recipe on page 49) with a crisp green salad.

Poultry

It's no wonder that chicken and turkey are so popular—they're naturally low in fat, economical, easy to cook, and impressively versatile.

Tender and juicy, chicken can be purchased whole or in parts, bone-in or boneless, and with or without skin. Nutritionists now believe that chicken has about the same fat content whether it's skinned before or after cooking, but in any case, the meat absorbs seasonings better if the skin is removed before the bird goes into the pot or onto the grill.

Turkey, like chicken, is widely available in many convenient and quick-to-prepare forms, ranging from whole or sliced breasts to individually packaged drumsticks and thighs to adaptable ground meat.

When you cook poultry, you'll want to choose a method that doesn't cancel out the lowfat advantage. When pan-frying, use a nonstick skillet and a minimum of fat (preferably an unsaturated vegetable oil; see page 101). Also try for as little fat as possible in the marinades you select for chicken or turkey to be broiled, barbecued, grilled, or stir-fried. If you mix ground chicken or turkey with egg to make burgers, meatballs, or meat loaf, use only the egg white; if necessary, moisten the mixture further with a few spoonfuls of low-sodium broth, a dollop of catsup or chili sauce, or a splash of wine.

Apple Country Chicken

Preparation time: About 15 minutes

Cooking time: About 40 minutes

This recipe comes from one of Washington's chief apple-growing districts, but the distinctive curry flavor calls up images of India. Accent the dish with a touch of tart yogurt, if you like.

1 teaspoon curry powder

1 large Golden Delicious apple (about 8 oz.), cored and chopped

1 large yellow onion, finely chopped

1 tablespoon lemon juice

4 ounces mushrooms, sliced

1 teaspoon chicken-flavored instant bouillon

2 cups apple juice or cider

3¼ to 3½ pounds chicken thighs, skinned and trimmed of fat

1 tablespoon all-purpose flour

2 tablespoons sliced green onion

½ cup plain lowfat yogurt (optional)

Place curry powder in a wide frying pan and stir over medium heat until slightly darker in color (3 to 4 minutes). Add apple, yellow onion, lemon juice, mushrooms, bouillon, and 1½ cups of the apple juice; bring to a boil.

Rinse chicken and pat dry; add to pan. Reduce heat, cover, and simmer until meat near bone is no longer pink; cut to test (about 30 minutes). Lift chicken from pan; arrange on a warm platter. Keep warm.

Blend flour and remaining ½ cup apple juice. Gradually add to sauce in pan, stirring; increase heat to high and cook, stirring, until sauce is thickened. Pour over chicken. Garnish with green onion; offer yogurt to add to taste, if desired. Makes 4 to 6 servings.

Per serving: 305 calories (22% fat, 31% carbohydrates, 47% protein), 7 g total fat (1.8 g saturated fat), 23 g carbohydrates, 36 g protein, 145 mg cholesterol, 348 mg sodium

Chicken & Mushrooms with Couscous

Preparation time: About 20 minutes

Cooking time: About 20 minutes

Mild, creamy, quick-cooking couscous is the perfect foil for tender stir-fried chicken in a cayenne-sparked sauce. Offer fresh asparagus spears alongside.

1 pound boneless, skinless chicken thighs, trimmed of fat

1 tablespoon margarine

1 large onion, finely chopped

12 ounces mushrooms, sliced

2 teaspoons cornstarch

1 cup low-sodium chicken broth

3 tablespoons dry sherry

2 tablespoons soy sauce

⅛ teaspoon ground red pepper (cayenne)

2 cups lowfat milk

1½ cups couscous

Vegetable oil cooking spray

Cilantro sprigs

Rinse chicken; pat dry. Place pieces between sheets of plastic wrap and pound with a flat-surfaced mallet until about ¼ inch thick; then cut chicken into ½-inch-wide strips. Set aside.

Melt margarine in a wide nonstick frying pan over medium-high heat. Add onion and mushrooms; cook, stirring often, until liquid has evaporated and onion is golden and sweet tasting (10 to 12 minutes).

Meanwhile, in a bowl, blend cornstarch and ¼ cup of the broth; stir in sherry, soy sauce, and red pepper. Set aside. In a 2-quart pan, bring milk and remaining ¾ cup broth to a boil. Stir in couscous; cover, remove from heat, and let stand for 10 minutes.

Remove onion mixture from frying pan and set aside. Spray pan with cooking spray and place over high heat. Add chicken and cook, lifting and stirring, until meat is tinged with brown and is no longer pink in center; cut to test (4 to 5 minutes). Return onion mixture to pan; add cornstarch mixture and cook, stirring constantly, until sauce is bubbly (about 1 minute). Fluff couscous with a fork, then mound on a warm platter; spoon chicken beside couscous. Garnish with cilantro sprigs. Makes 4 to 6 servings.

Per serving: 434 calories (17% fat, 54% carbohydrates, 29% protein), 8 g total fat (2 g saturated fat), 56 g carbohydrates, 31 g protein, 79 mg cholesterol, 586 mg sodium

■ *Pictured on page 46*

Chicken Vermicelli Carbonara

Preparation time: About 25 minutes

Cooking time: About 30 minutes

Here's a creative lowfat version of an Italian classic. Chicken stands in for the usual pork; chopped onion, braised and deglazed in fennel-seasoned broth, adds a rich, browned flavor.

   1 **large onion, finely chopped**
   ½ **teaspoon fennel seeds**
1¾ **cups low-sodium chicken broth**
  12 **to 14 ounces boneless, skinless chicken thighs, trimmed of fat and cut into ½-inch chunks**
   1 **cup finely chopped parsley**
   3 **egg whites (about 6 tablespoons)**
   1 **egg**
  12 **ounces to 1 pound dry vermicelli**
1½ **cups (about 6 oz.) finely shredded Parmesan cheese**
     Salt and freshly ground pepper

In a wide nonstick frying pan, combine onion, fennel seeds, and 1 cup of the broth. Bring to a boil; boil, stirring occasionally, until liquid has evaporated. Continue to cook until browned bits accumulate in pan; then add water, 2 tablespoons at a time, stirring until all browned bits are loosened. Continue to cook until mixture begins to brown again; repeat deglazing, using 2 tablespoons water each time, until onions are a uniformly light golden brown color.

To pan, add chicken and 2 tablespoons more water. Cook, stirring, until drippings begin to brown; deglaze pan with 2 tablespoons water. When pan is dry, add remaining ¾ cup broth; bring to a boil. Add parsley; keep warm over lowest heat. In a bowl, beat egg whites and egg to blend; set aside.

In a 6-quart pan, cook vermicelli in 4 quarts boiling water just until tender to bite (8 to 10 minutes); or cook according to package directions. Drain well.

Add hot pasta to pan with chicken. Pour egg mixture over pasta and at once begin lifting with 2 forks to mix well (eggs cook if you delay mixing); add 1 cup of the cheese as you mix. Pour mixture onto a warm deep platter and continue to mix until almost all broth is absorbed. Season to taste with remaining ½ cup cheese, salt, and pepper. Makes 6 to 8 servings.

Per serving: 408 calories (24% fat, 46% carbohydrates, 30% protein), 11 g total fat (5 g saturated fat), 46 g carbohydrates, 30 g protein, 93 mg cholesterol, 491 mg sodium

Devilishly Spicy Chicken

Preparation time: About 15 minutes

Cooking time: About 1 hour

Simmered in beer and chili sauce and seasoned with plenty of dry mustard, these chicken pieces are decidedly piquant in flavor. To balance the heat, stir sweet-tasting peas into the cooking pan at the last minute.

   1 **chicken (about 4 lbs.), cut up and skinned**
   2 **tablespoons margarine**
   2 **medium-size onions, chopped**
   1 **tablespoon dry mustard**
   1 **can or bottle (about 12 oz.) beer**
   ⅓ **cup tomato-based chili sauce**
   3 **tablespoons Worcestershire**
   4 **cups hot cooked eggless noodles**
   1 **package (about 10 oz.) frozen tiny peas, thawed**

Rinse chicken, pat dry, and set aside.

Melt margarine in a wide frying pan over medium-high heat. Add onions and cook, stirring often, until golden brown (12 to 15 minutes). Stir in mustard; then add beer, chili sauce, and Worcestershire. Add all chicken pieces except breasts; turn to coat. Reduce heat, cover, and simmer for 20 minutes. Turn chicken over, add breasts to pan, cover, and continue to simmer until meat near thighbone is no longer pink; cut to test (about 20 more minutes).

Spoon noodles onto a warm platter; top with chicken and keep warm. Bring cooking liquid to a boil; boil, stirring, until reduced to 2 cups (6 to 8 minutes). Add peas; stir just until hot (about 1 minute). Spoon sauce over chicken. Makes 4 to 6 servings.

Per serving: 411 calories (24% fat, 32% carbohydrates, 44% protein), 11 g total fat (2 g saturated fat), 32 g carbohydrates, 45 g protein, 122 mg cholesterol, 617 mg sodium

■ *Pictured on facing page*

Sesame Chicken with Stir-fried Vegetables

Preparation time: About 20 minutes

Cooking time: 12 to 15 minutes

A bed of stir-fried red cabbage and emerald snow peas provides a crisp, colorful contrast to these grilled chicken breasts sprinkled with sesame seeds.

    4 chicken breast halves (about 2 lbs. *total*),
       skinned and boned
    1 teaspoon sesame seeds
       Vegetable oil cooking spray
    4 teaspoons *each* rice vinegar and soy sauce
 1½ teaspoons Oriental sesame oil
    1 tablespoon grated fresh ginger
    2 cloves garlic, minced or pressed
  ½ teaspoon sugar
    1 tablespoon vegetable oil
    8 ounces mushrooms, sliced
    4 cups thinly sliced red cabbage
    4 ounces Chinese pea pods (also called
       snow peas), ends and strings removed
    2 cups hot cooked rice

Rinse chicken, pat dry, and sprinkle with sesame seeds. Spray a ridged cooktop grill pan with cooking spray. Place over medium heat and preheat until a drop of water dances on surface. Then place chicken on grill and cook, turning once, until well browned on outside and no longer pink in thickest part; cut to test (12 to 15 minutes).

Meanwhile, in a small bowl, stir together vinegar, soy sauce, sesame oil, ginger, garlic, and sugar; set aside. Then heat vegetable oil in a wide nonstick frying pan over medium-high heat. Add mushrooms and cook, stirring often, for about 3 minutes. Add cabbage and cook, stirring often, until it begins to soften (about 2 minutes). Add pea pods and cook, stirring, just until they turn bright green (1 to 2 minutes). Add vinegar mixture and stir for 1 more minute.

Divide vegetables among 4 warm dinner plates. Cut each chicken piece diagonally across the grain into ½-inch-wide strips. Arrange chicken over vegetables; serve with rice. Makes 4 servings.

Per serving: 400 calories (19% fat, 40% carbohydrates, 41% protein), 8 g total fat (1 g saturated fat), 40 g carbohydrates, 40 g protein, 86 mg cholesterol, 454 mg sodium

Sautéed Balsamic Chicken with Fettuccine

Preparation time: About 15 minutes, plus about 20 minutes to soak mushrooms

Cooking time: About 20 minutes

When you make this savory entrée, use a light, fruity red wine, such as a Beaujolais, in the sauce.

  ½ ounce (about ½ cup) dried mushrooms
    4 chicken breast halves (about 2 lbs. *total*),
       skinned and boned
       Freshly ground pepper
       About 1 tablespoon all-purpose flour
    2 teaspoons olive oil
    3 cloves garlic, minced or pressed
    3 small pear-shaped (Roma-type) tomatoes
       (about 6 oz. *total*), chopped
  ½ cup *each* beef broth and dry red wine
  ¼ cup balsamic or red wine vinegar
    1 teaspoon cornstarch
    1 tablespoon cold water
    1 package (9 or 10 oz.) fresh fettuccine,
       cooked and drained (keep hot)

Soak mushrooms in hot water to cover until soft (about 20 minutes); drain, reserving ½ cup of the liquid. Cut off and discard tough mushroom stems.

Rinse chicken; pat dry. Sprinkle with pepper; dust with flour. Heat oil in a wide nonstick frying pan over medium-high heat. Add chicken; cook, turning once, until well browned on both sides. Lift chicken from pan; set aside. Add garlic, tomatoes, and mushrooms to pan; stir for 1 minute. Add reserved ½ cup mushroom liquid, broth, wine, and 3 tablespoons of the vinegar. Boil for 3 minutes; remove from heat.

Blend cornstarch and water; stir into sauce in pan. Return chicken to pan, spooning sauce over it. Return to medium-low heat, cover, and cook until meat in thickest part is no longer pink; cut to test (10 to 12 minutes). Stir remaining 1 tablespoon vinegar into sauce. Pour fettuccine onto a warm deep platter; top with chicken and sauce. Makes 4 servings.

Per serving: 414 calories (13% fat, 44% carbohydrates, 43% protein), 6 g total fat (1 g saturated fat), 45 g carbohydrates, 44 g protein, 165 mg cholesterol, 224 mg sodium

Easy to put together in a hurry, *Sesame Chicken with*
Stir-fried Vegetables (recipe on facing page) offers a delicious example
of the fresh California style of lowfat cooking. Accompany the bright vegetable
medley and tender meat with hot, fluffy rice.

Roasted Thai Turkey Nuggets

Preparation time: About 15 minutes

Baking time: 10 to 12 minutes

Here's a way to brown chunks of skinned turkey breast without adding many calories. You coat the meat in a spicy blend of garlic, pepper, and cilantro, then bake briefly in a hot oven. Serve the tender nuggets with a Thai-inspired sweet-sour sauce.

1 **pound boneless, skinless turkey breast**

3 **tablespoons minced cilantro**

2 **teaspoons coarsely ground pepper**

8 **cloves garlic, minced or pressed**

⅓ **cup canned tomato sauce**

1 **tablespoon distilled white or cider vinegar**

1 **tablespoon firmly packed brown sugar**

½ **cup raisins**

Rinse turkey, pat dry, and cut into 8 equal-size pieces (no more than 1½ inches thick). Mix cilantro, pepper, and 6 cloves of the garlic; pat mixture over turkey pieces, covering all sides. Place pieces well apart in a shallow rimmed baking pan. Bake in a 500° oven until meat is lightly browned on outside and no longer pink in center; cut to test (10 to 12 minutes).

Meanwhile, in a food processor or blender, combine remaining 2 cloves garlic, tomato sauce, vinegar, sugar, and raisins; whirl until raisins are chopped. Offer raisin sauce to spoon over turkey to taste. Makes 4 servings.

Per serving: 215 calories (8% fat, 40% carbohydrates, 52% protein), 2 g total fat (1 g saturated fat), 22 g carbohydrates, 28 g protein, 70 mg cholesterol, 203 mg sodium

Turkey & Mushroom Burgers

Preparation time: About 15 minutes

Cooking time: 8 to 10 minutes

Feel free to lavish these lean turkey-breast burgers with such favorite trimmings as tomato slices, mustard, lettuce, and dill pickles—none will add a significant amount of fat. In place of the usual French fries or chips, offer Garlic Potatoes (page 76) as a side dish.

1 **egg white (about 2 tablespoons)**

¼ **cup dry white wine**

⅓ **cup soft French bread crumbs**

¼ **teaspoon salt**

⅛ **teaspoon pepper**

¼ **cup finely chopped shallots**

1 **pound ground turkey breast**

4 **ounces mushrooms, finely chopped**
   Olive oil cooking spray

6 **onion hamburger rolls, split and warmed**
   Condiments: Sliced tomatoes, Dijon mustard, rinsed and crisped lettuce leaves, and/or sliced dill pickles (optional)

In a medium-size bowl, beat egg white and wine until blended. Stir in crumbs, salt, pepper, and shallots; then lightly mix in turkey and mushrooms. Shape turkey mixture into 6 patties, each about ½ inch thick.

Spray a wide nonstick frying pan with cooking spray. Place over medium-high heat; add turkey patties. Cook, turning once, until patties are lightly browned on both sides and juices run clear when a knife is inserted in center (8 to 10 minutes). Serve on warm rolls; add condiments to taste, if desired. Makes 6 servings.

Per serving: 234 calories (15% fat, 45% carbohydrates, 40% protein), 4 g total fat (1 g saturated fat), 25 g carbohydrates, 22 g protein, 49 mg cholesterol, 369 mg sodium

■ *Pictured on page 11*

Moussaka Dubrovnik

Preparation time: About 30 minutes

Cooking time: About 1½ hours

For an ideal make-ahead dinner, try this streamlined version of a famous eggplant casserole. The eggplant slices are oven-browned, not fried; the meat sauce is a spicy, super-lean blend of ground turkey breast, garlic, and browned onions. And in place of the traditional cream sauce, we've used a simple combination of broth and light sour cream.

2	**large eggplants (2½ to 3 lbs. *total*)**
	Olive oil cooking spray
2	**large onions, finely chopped**
1	**clove garlic, minced or pressed**
2	**teaspoons olive oil**
1	**cup water**
1½	**pounds boneless, skinless turkey breast, cut into 1-inch chunks**
¼	**teaspoon *each* fennel seeds, ground cinnamon, ground cumin, and ground cardamom**
	About ⅛ teaspoon freshly grated or ground nutmeg
3	**tablespoons plus 1 teaspoon cornstarch**
3	**cups low-sodium chicken broth**
	Salt and pepper
½	**cup light sour cream or plain nonfat yogurt**
2	**tablespoons grated Parmesan cheese (optional)**

Cut unpeeled eggplants lengthwise into ½-inch-thick slices. Spray 2 shallow rimmed baking pans with cooking spray. Divide eggplant slices equally between pans in a single layer, overlapping slices slightly; spray eggplant with cooking spray. Bake in a 450° oven for 20 minutes; turn slices over and continue to bake until lightly browned and very soft when pressed (about 10 more minutes). Line a 9- by 13- by 2-inch casserole with half the eggplant; set remaining pan of eggplant aside.

To empty baking pan, add onions, garlic, oil, and ½ cup of the water. Bake until water has evaporated and onions are dark brown, stirring often with a wide spatula (30 to 35 minutes). Meanwhile, whirl turkey in a food processor, about half at a time, until minced.

Add remaining ½ cup water to onion mixture, stirring to scrape up browned bits. Scatter turkey over onion mixture. Return to oven and bake until turkey is opaque throughout (about 6 minutes). Set turkey mixture aside.

In a 2-quart pan, mix fennel seeds, cinnamon, cumin, cardamom, ⅛ teaspoon of the nutmeg, and 4 teaspoons of the cornstarch. Blend in 1½ cups of the broth. Bring to a boil over high heat, stirring constantly; stir into turkey mixture. Season to taste with salt and pepper.

Spread turkey mixture over eggplant in casserole. Cover with remaining eggplant; set aside.

Rinse the 2-quart pan; in it, smoothly blend remaining 2 tablespoons cornstarch and ¼ cup of the broth. Blend in sour cream, then remaining 1¼ cups broth. Bring to a boil over high heat, stirring. Spoon over eggplant. (At this point, you may cover and refrigerate for up to a day.)

Sprinkle casserole with cheese, if used; then sprinkle lightly with nutmeg. Bake, uncovered, in a 425° oven until heated through (15 to 20 minutes; 30 to 40 minutes if refrigerated). Makes 8 to 10 servings.

Per serving: 190 calories (23% fat, 33% carbohydrates, 44% protein), 5 g total fat (2 g saturated fat), 16 g carbohydrates, 21 g protein, 51 mg cholesterol, 75 mg sodium

*Celebrate springtime with a fresh and elegant entrée:
Balsamic-broiled Salmon with Mint (recipe on page 57). To complement
the succulent fillets and steamed red potatoes, you might offer crusty
French bread and a blush wine such as a Zinfandel rosé.*

Seafood

Both fish and shellfish offer good eating with relatively little fat or cholesterol. The fat these foods do contain is mainly polyunsaturated and monounsaturated (see page 101); some fish have a unique polyunsaturated fatty acid called omega-3, believed to be helpful in reducing blood clots, lowering blood cholesterol, and preventing heart disease. The cholesterol levels of most fish are comparable to those of poultry breast and lean red meats. Shrimp, while low in fat, are almost six times higher in cholesterol than scallops; if you have been advised to limit your cholesterol intake, serve shrimp no more than once a week.

For best results, buy only fresh seafood—and cook it on the day of purchase, if possible. Truly fresh fish fillets and steaks look moist and cleanly cut; they have a firm, elastic texture and the clean aroma of an ocean breeze. If seafood smells disagreeable, don't buy it.

Successful seafood cookery depends to a great extent on learning to judge doneness: most fish and shellfish cook quickly and can rapidly become dry and flavorless if over-cooked. To test, cut a small slit in the center of a fillet, steak, or whole fish; the flesh should look just barely opaque but still moist. Crab, lobster, scallops, and shrimp should also be opaque but still moist in the center; oysters, clams, and mussels are done when their shells pop open.

Halibut with Tomato-Cilantro Linguine

Preparation time: About 10 minutes

Cooking time: 6 to 8 minutes

This quick, stylish dish is just right for a summer's evening. While you sauté the halibut steaks, also cook some fresh linguine; then top both fish and pasta with a fresh-tasting room-temperature tomato sauce.

> 2 tablespoons olive oil
>
> 1½ tablespoons lime juice
>
> 1 tablespoon drained capers
>
> 4 small pear-shaped (Roma-type) tomatoes (about 8 oz. *total*), at room temperature, seeded and chopped
>
> 2 cloves garlic, minced or pressed
>
> ¼ teaspoon ground red pepper (cayenne)
>
> ⅓ cup cilantro leaves
>
> 1¼ to 1½ pounds halibut steaks or other white-fleshed fish steaks such as sea bass (about ¾ inch thick)
>
> Salt and black pepper
>
> Olive oil cooking spray
>
> 1 package (9 or 10 oz.) fresh linguine

In a large bowl, stir together oil, lime juice, capers, tomatoes, garlic, red pepper, and cilantro; set aside. Remove and discard any skin from fish, then rinse fish and pat dry. Cut fish into 4 serving-size pieces; season to taste with salt and black pepper.

Spray a wide nonstick frying pan with cooking spray; place over medium-high heat. Add fish and cook, turning once, until lightly browned on outside and just opaque but still moist in thickest part; cut to test (6 to 8 minutes).

Meanwhile, in a 5- to 6-quart pan, cook linguine in 3 quarts boiling water just until tender to bite (1 to 2 minutes); or cook according to package directions. Drain pasta well. Set 2 tablespoons of the tomato mixture aside; lightly mix remaining mixture with hot pasta.

Divide pasta among 4 warm plates; top each serving with a piece of fish, then top fish evenly with reserved tomato mixture. Makes 4 servings.

Per serving: 442 calories (25% fat, 37% carbohydrates, 38% protein), 12 g total fat (1 g saturated fat), 40 g carbohydrates, 42 g protein, 129 mg cholesterol, 163 mg sodium

Poached Fish with Fennel & Tomato

Preparation time: About 10 minutes

Cooking time: 40 to 45 minutes

You can prepare these brightly sauced poached fish fillets even when you're in a hurry. Serve with crusty bread, a salad of mixed baby lettuces, and a dry white wine such as Sauvignon Blanc.

> 2 bulbs fennel (about 12 oz. *total*)
>
> 1½ tablespoons olive oil
>
> 1 medium-size onion, thinly sliced
>
> 1 clove garlic, minced or pressed
>
> ¼ teaspoon fennel seeds
>
> 1 large can (about 28 oz.) diced tomatoes
>
> 1 cup dry white wine
>
> 1¼ to 1½ pounds lingcod or rockfish fillets (about 1 inch thick)
>
> Salt and pepper

Rinse fennel well; trim and discard bulb bases and any discolored or bruised portions. Cut off and discard coarse tops of stalks, reserving a few of the green leaves for garnish. Cut bulbs lengthwise into quarters; thinly slice quarters crosswise.

Heat oil in a 5- to 6-quart pan over medium-low heat. Add sliced fennel and onion; cook, stirring often, until onion is pale golden (8 to 10 minutes). Add garlic, fennel seeds, tomatoes and their liquid, and wine. Bring to a gentle boil, then cook until sauce is reduced to about 4 cups (20 to 25 minutes). Meanwhile, rinse fish and cut into 4 serving-size pieces.

Add fish to reduced tomato sauce. Reduce heat, cover, and simmer until fish is just opaque but still moist in thickest part; cut to test (about 10 minutes). Transfer fish to 4 shallow bowls; stir sauce to blend, then spoon over fish. Garnish with reserved fennel leaves and season to taste with salt and pepper. Makes 4 servings.

Per serving: 239 calories (28% fat, 21% carbohydrates, 51% protein), 7 g total fat (1 g saturated fat), 13 g carbohydrates, 31 g protein, 81 mg cholesterol, 488 mg sodium

■ Pictured on page 54

Balsamic-broiled Salmon with Mint

Preparation time: About 15 minutes

Cooking time: About 25 minutes

Warmed by the heat of salmon fillets broiled just on one side, a generous sprinkling of fresh mint adds a refreshing note to this elegant, sweet-sour entrée.

1¼	**pounds small red thin-skinned potatoes** (*each* **1½ to 2 inches in diameter), scrubbed**
3	**tablespoons balsamic or raspberry vinegar**
1½	**tablespoons honey**
¾	**teaspoon salad oil**
1	**to 1¼ pounds salmon fillets (¾ inch thick)**
½	**cup fresh mint leaves, minced**
	Mint sprigs
	Lemon slices

Peel a 1-inch-wide strip around center of each potato. Steam potatoes, covered, on a rack above about 1 inch of boiling water until tender when pierced (about 25 minutes).

Meanwhile, in a small bowl, stir together vinegar, honey, and oil. Then remove and discard any skin from salmon; rinse salmon and pat dry. Cut salmon into 4 serving-size pieces; place, skinned sides down, in a lightly greased shallow rimmed baking pan. Drizzle salmon with half the vinegar mixture. Broil about 6 inches below heat, brushing several times with remaining vinegar mixture, until just opaque but still moist in thickest part; cut to test (8 to 10 minutes).

Transfer salmon to a warm platter; drizzle with any cooking juices. Surround with potatoes. Sprinkle salmon and potatoes with minced mint; garnish with mint sprigs and lemon slices. Makes 4 servings.

Per serving: 332 calories (25% fat, 40% carbohydrates, 35% protein), 9 g total fat (1 g saturated fat), 33 g carbohydrates, 28 g protein, 71 mg cholesterol, 68 mg sodium

Grilled Tuna with Tomato-Orange Relish

Preparation time: About 10 minutes

Cooking time: About 30 minutes

The pungent crimson relish that accompanies these garlicky grilled tuna steaks also goes well with other fish and chicken cooked on the barbecue.

	Tomato-Orange Relish (recipe follows)
1	**teaspoon olive oil**
2	**cloves garlic, minced or pressed**
2	**tablespoons lemon juice**
6	**boneless, skinless tuna steaks (about 6 oz. each), ¾ to 1 inch thick**
	Freshly ground pepper
	Italian parsley sprigs
	Orange slices

Prepare Tomato-Orange Relish.

Mix oil, garlic, and lemon juice. Rinse tuna, pat dry, and brush all over with oil mixture. Place tuna on a greased grill 4 to 6 inches above a solid bed of hot coals. Cook, turning once, until browned on outside but still pale pink in center; cut to test (3 to 5 minutes).

Transfer tuna to a warm platter; season to taste with pepper. Garnish with parsley sprigs and orange slices. Spoon a dollop of Tomato-Orange Relish over each piece of tuna; serve with remaining relish to add to taste. Makes 6 servings.

■ *Tomato-Orange Relish.* Grate ½ teaspoon peel (colored part only) from 1 small **orange;** set grated peel aside. Cut remaining peel and all white membrane from orange; cut fruit into chunks. In a food processor or blender, combine 2 medium-size **tomatoes** (about 12 oz. *total*), coarsely chopped; 1 tablespoon *each* **tomato paste** and **cider vinegar;** and chopped orange. Whirl until coarsely puréed; set aside.

Spray a 1½- to 2-quart pan with **vegetable oil cooking spray.** Add 1 **small dried hot red chile** and ½ teaspoon *each* **mustard seeds** and **cumin seeds;** stir over medium-high heat until seeds begin to pop (about 2 minutes). Mix in ¼ teaspoon **ground allspice,** 2 tablespoons firmly packed **brown sugar,** ¼ cup **raisins,** tomato mixture, and grated orange peel. Cook, stirring, until sugar is dissolved. Reduce heat so mixture cooks at a gentle boil; cook, stirring often, until consistency is jamlike (20 to 25 minutes). Remove chile, if desired. Serve hot or at room temperature.

Per serving: 474 calories (28% fat, 20% carbohydrates, 52% protein), 14 g total fat (3 g saturated fat), 23 g carbohydrates, 61 g protein, 97 mg cholesterol, 144 mg sodium

Citrus Lingcod with Orange Almond Rice

Preparation time: About 30 minutes

Cooking time: 30 to 35 minutes

A quartet of citrus fruits goes into the sauce for broiled lingcod and fragrant rice in this glamorous treatment of a notably lean fish.

>   4   medium-size oranges (about 2 lbs. *total*)
>   1   large pink grapefruit (about 12 oz.)
>   1   *each* medium-size lemon and lime
>   ¼   cup slivered almonds
>   2   tablespoons olive oil
>   6   tablespoons chopped shallots
> 2¼   cups water
>   ¼   teaspoon almond extract
> 1½   cups long-grain white rice
>   2   pounds lingcod fillets (about 1 inch thick)
>   Olive oil cooking spray
>   ¼   cup rice vinegar or white wine vinegar

Finely shred 1½ tablespoons *each* orange and grapefruit peel (colored part only) and 1 teaspoon *each* lemon and lime peel (colored part only). Mix peels and set aside.

Cut remaining peel and all white membrane from grapefruit, lemon, lime, and 2 of the oranges. Hold each peeled fruit over a bowl; cut between membrane to release fruit segments into bowl. Set aside. Squeeze juice from remaining 2 oranges; set aside.

Toast almonds in a 2-quart pan over medium heat until golden (3 to 5 minutes), stirring often. Remove from pan; set aside. In same pan, heat 1 tablespoon of the oil; add ¼ cup of the shallots and cook, stirring, until soft but not browned (2 to 3 minutes). Add water, ¾ cup of the orange juice, and almond extract. Bring to a boil; add rice. Reduce heat to low, cover, and simmer until rice is tender to bite (20 to 25 minutes).

Meanwhile, rinse fish and pat dry; cut into serving-size pieces. Spray with cooking spray. Place fish on lightly greased rack of a broiler pan. Broil about 4 inches below heat, turning once, until fish is just opaque but still moist in thickest part; cut to test (about 10 minutes).

While fish is broiling, heat remaining 1 tablespoon oil in a wide nonstick frying pan over medium heat. Add vinegar, remaining 2 tablespoons shallots, any remaining orange juice, and citrus segments and juices. Cook, swirling pan often, just until sauce is warm.

Stir almonds into rice; spoon onto warm plates. Lift fish onto plates; spoon sauce over fish and rice. Garnish with mixed citrus peels. Makes 4 to 6 servings.

Per serving: 541 calories (19% fat, 52% carbohydrates, 29% protein), 12 g total fat (2 g saturated fat), 71 g carbohydrates, 39 g protein, 94 mg cholesterol, 113 mg sodium

Grilled Scallops with Pear-Ginger Coulis

Preparation time: About 15 minutes

Cooking time: About 20 minutes

A tart, gingery purée of fresh pears makes a saucy dip for skewered sea scallops cooked on the barbecue.

>   4   teaspoons olive oil
>   1   small onion, chopped
>   2   tablespoons chopped fresh ginger
>   3   medium-size firm-ripe pears (1¼ to 1½ lbs. *total*), peeled, cored, and diced
>   ¼   cup rice vinegar or white wine vinegar
>   1   pound sea scallops, rinsed and patted dry

Heat 1 tablespoon of the oil in a 2-quart pan over medium-high heat. Add onion and cook, stirring often, until soft but not browned (3 to 5 minutes). Add ginger, pears, and vinegar. Cook, stirring occasionally, until pears are tender when pierced (12 to 15 minutes). Transfer mixture to a food processor or blender; whirl until smoothly puréed. Return to pan and keep warm over lowest heat.

Meanwhile, cut scallops in half horizontally, if necessary, to make ½-inch-thick discs. Lightly mix scallops and remaining 1 teaspoon oil. Thread a fourth of the scallops on each of 4 metal skewers, piercing scallops horizontally (through diameter) so they lie flat.

Place skewers on a greased grill 4 to 6 inches above a solid bed of hot coals. Cook, turning once, until scallops are opaque in center; cut to test (5 to 7 minutes). Spoon a fourth of the warm pear mixture on each of 4 warm dinner plates; lay a scallop skewer alongside. Makes 4 servings.

Per serving: 240 calories (22% fat, 46% carbohydrates, 32% protein), 6 g total fat (1 g saturated fat), 28 g carbohydrates, 20 g protein, 37 mg cholesterol, 183 mg sodium

Orange, grapefruit, lemon, and lime all go into Citrus Lingcod with Orange Almond Rice (recipe on facing page). Lean and lovely to look at, it's a delightful choice for a special meal. Alongside the fish, serve tender green asparagus spears.

Mexican Shellfish Chowder

Preparation time: About 45 minutes

Cooking time: About 45 minutes

You might call this hearty seafood soup a Mexican-style bouillabaisse. For the fish, you can use all one kind or a combination of two or more types.

- 2½ quarts low-sodium chicken broth
- ½ cup dry white wine
- 1 bay leaf
- 2 cloves garlic, minced or pressed
- ⅛ teaspoon powdered saffron
- 4 to 6 small fresh jalapeño chiles, seeded and finely chopped
- 3 large tomatoes (1¼ to 1½ lbs. *total*), chopped
- 2 pounds white-fleshed fish steaks or fillets such as rockfish, halibut, or lingcod
- 8 ounces sea scallops, rinsed and patted dry
- 18 small hard-shell clams suitable for steaming, scrubbed
- 8 ounces medium-large raw shrimp (36 to 42 per lb.), shelled and deveined

Salt and pepper
- ¼ cup chopped cilantro
  Lime wedges

In a 6- to 8-quart pan, combine broth, wine, bay leaf, garlic, saffron, and chiles. Cover and bring to a boil over medium-high heat; reduce heat and simmer for 30 minutes. Meanwhile, in a food processor or blender, whirl tomatoes until coarsely puréed; set aside. Rinse fish, pat dry, and cut into chunks. Cut scallops into ½-inch-thick slices.

Stir tomatoes into broth mixture. Cover, increase heat to medium, and bring to a boil. Add clams, reduce heat to medium-low, cover, and simmer for 5 minutes. Add fish, scallops, and shrimp. Cover and simmer until clams pop open and fish, scallops, and shrimp are opaque in center; cut to test (3 to 5 minutes). Season to taste with salt and pepper; sprinkle with cilantro. Serve with lime wedges to squeeze into soup to taste. Makes 8 to 10 servings.

Per serving: 204 calories (19% fat, 14% carbohydrates, 67% protein), 4 g total fat (1 g saturated fat), 7 g carbohydrates, 33 g protein, 81 mg cholesterol, 208 mg sodium

Shrimp & Pea Pod Stir-fry

Preparation time: About 30 minutes

Cooking time: About 10 minutes

Serve this colorful, saucy mélange of pink shrimp and tender-crisp snow peas atop a bed of fluffy rice. For a change, you might serve fiber-rich brown rice or fragrant basmati rice in place of the usual long- or short-grain white variety.

- 2 tablespoons soy sauce
- 1 tablespoon finely chopped fresh ginger
- ¼ cup dry sherry or water
- ¼ cup rice vinegar or white wine vinegar
- 1½ teaspoons cornstarch
- 2 tablespoons salad oil
- 1 cup sliced mushrooms
- 1 clove garlic, minced or pressed
- 1 pound medium-size raw shrimp (40 to 45 per lb.), shelled and deveined
- 4 ounces Chinese pea pods (also called snow peas), ends and strings removed

- 3 cups hot cooked rice
- ¼ cup thinly sliced green onions

In a small bowl, stir together soy sauce, ginger, sherry, vinegar, and cornstarch; set aside.

Heat 1 tablespoon of the oil in a wide nonstick frying pan or wok over high heat. Add mushrooms and cook, stirring, until lightly browned (about 4 minutes). Stir in garlic, then spoon mixture into a bowl; set aside.

Heat remaining 1 tablespoon oil in pan. Then add shrimp and cook, stirring, until opaque in center; cut to test (about 3 minutes). Return mushroom mixture to pan; add pea pods and soy sauce mixture. Cook, stirring constantly, until pea pods turn bright green and sauce comes to a boil (1 to 2 minutes). Spoon rice onto a warm deep platter; top with shrimp mixture and garnish with onions. Makes 4 servings.

Per serving: 410 calories (21% fat, 53% carbohydrates, 26% protein), 9 g total fat (1 g saturated fat), 51 g carbohydrates, 25 g protein, 140 mg cholesterol, 657 mg sodium

Scallops & Spinach Pasta

Preparation time: About 10 minutes

Cooking time: About 10 minutes

The white, red, and green colors of the Italian flag may have inspired this robust combination of snowy scallops, ripe tomatoes, and spinach fettuccine. Serve with an Italian white wine such as Verdicchio or with a California Sauvignon Blanc.

- 8 ounces dry green fettuccine or 1 package (9 oz.) fresh green fettuccine
- 2 tablespoons pine nuts
- 2 tablespoons olive oil
- 1 pound bay scallops, rinsed and patted dry
- 2 cloves garlic, minced or pressed
- 1 large tomato (about 8 oz.), seeded and chopped
- ¼ cup dry white wine
- ¼ cup chopped Italian parsley
  Salt and freshly ground pepper

In a 5- to 6-quart pan, cook fettuccine in 3 quarts boiling water just until tender to bite (8 to 10 minutes for dry pasta, 3 to 4 minutes for fresh); or cook according to package directions. Drain well.

While pasta is cooking, toast pine nuts in a wide nonstick frying pan over medium-low heat until lightly browned (about 3 minutes), stirring often. Remove nuts from pan and set aside. Then heat oil in pan over medium-high heat. Add scallops and cook, turning often with a wide spatula, until opaque in center; cut to test (2 to 3 minutes). Lift from pan, place on a warm plate, and keep warm.

Add garlic to pan; cook, stirring, just until it begins to brown (1 to 2 minutes). Stir in tomato, then wine; bring to a full boil. Remove pan from heat and add pasta, scallops and any accumulated liquid, and parsley; mix lightly, using 2 spoons. Season to taste with salt and pepper. Sprinkle with pine nuts. Makes 4 servings.

Per serving: 420 calories (28% fat, 44% carbohydrates, 28% protein), 13 g total fat (2 g saturated fat), 46 g carbohydrates, 29 g protein, 91 mg cholesterol, 229 mg sodium

Stir-fried Cracked Crab with Green Onions

Preparation time: About 20 minutes

Cooking time: 10 to 12 minutes

Dungeness crab heated in a flavorful blend of sherry, ginger, and oyster sauce makes a festive, delightfully messy main dish for an impromptu dinner party. You start with cooked shellfish from the market; if you're lucky, your seafood dealer will even clean and crack it for you. Complete the repast with a green salad and crusty bread—and be sure to provide finger bowls and plenty of napkins.

- ⅓ cup *each* dry sherry and water
- ¼ cup oyster sauce
- 2 teaspoons cornstarch
- 1 tablespoon salad oil
- 3 tablespoons finely chopped fresh ginger
- 14 green onions, cut into 2-inch lengths
- 3 large cooked Dungeness crabs (about 6 lbs. *total*), cleaned and cracked

In a small bowl, stir together sherry, water, oyster sauce, and cornstarch; set aside.

Heat oil in an 8- to 10-quart pan over high heat. Add ginger and white parts of onions; cook, stirring, just until onions begin to brown (about 2 minutes). Add sherry mixture and bring to a boil, stirring constantly (about 1 minute). Add crab pieces and green parts of onions; stir to coat with sauce. Reduce heat to low, cover, and cook, stirring occasionally, just until crab is heated through (5 to 8 minutes). Mound crab pieces on a warm large platter. Makes 6 servings.

Per serving: 147 calories (21% fat, 21% carbohydrates, 58% protein), 3 g total fat (0.4 g saturated fat), 8 g carbohydrates, 21 g protein, 64 mg cholesterol, 799 mg sodium

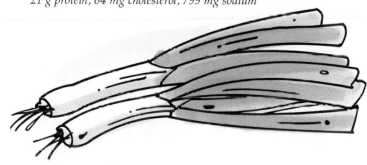

Bright colors, savory flavors, and abundant crunch explain the appeal of peanut-sprinkled Wild Spanish Rice (recipe on page 73). To complement this vegetarian main dish, serve warm corn muffins and a medley of grilled zucchini and golden pattypan squash.

Vegetarian Entrées

Everyone knows that vegetables and fruits taste good. And as generations of parents have stressed, they're also good for you: high in minerals, vitamins, and fiber, free of cholesterol, low in sodium, and—with a few exceptions— low in fat. Though usually cast in a supporting role, fresh produce can costar with pasta, grains, and legumes to make creative, often economical main dishes that are rich in both fiber and complex carbohydrates.

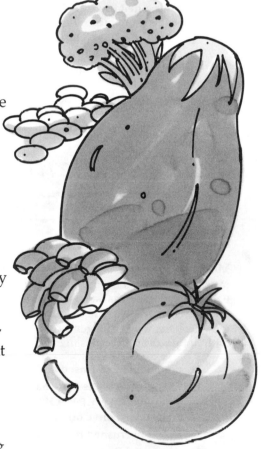

Protein from vegetable sources is generally incomplete—lacking one or more of the essential amino acids. To put together meals that provide complete protein, you'll need to combine grains and legumes, either in the same dish or in complementary individual dishes. Eggs and dairy products can also complete the nutritional picture. To keep total fat to a minimum, use these foods in modest amounts, and select milk products containing only one to two percent (or less) milk fat—nonfat or lowfat milk, evaporated skim milk, and nonfat or lowfat yogurt. Among cheeses, look for part-skim ricotta and mozzarella as well as other reduced-fat types; a number of varieties are now available, including Swiss and Cheddar.

Spaghetti alla Calabrese

Preparation time: About 25 minutes, plus 1 hour to soak tomatoes

Cooking time: About 30 minutes

In Calabria—a region at the "toe" of boot-shaped Italy—local produce plays a major role in many traditional dishes. This bright sauce combines dried tomatoes with a variety of fresh vegetables; it's good over spaghetti or other pasta. Adjust the number of piquant peperoncini to suit your taste.

- ⅓ **cup dried tomatoes**
- 2 **tablespoons olive oil**
- 1 **medium-size onion, chopped**
- 3 **cloves garlic, minced or pressed**
- 1 **medium-size carrot (about 3 oz.), diced**
- 1 **small red or yellow bell pepper (about 5 oz.), seeded and finely chopped**
- 8 **ounces mushrooms, thinly sliced**
- 1 **cup finely diced unpeeled eggplant**
- 2 **to 4 canned peperoncini peppers, drained, seeded, and minced**
- 1 **pound pear-shaped (Roma-type) tomatoes, cut lengthwise into eighths**
- 2 **small zucchini (about 5 oz. *total*), thinly sliced**
- 6 **large pitted ripe olives, thinly sliced**

- 1 **pound dry spaghetti**
  Salt and pepper
  Grated Parmesan cheese (optional)

Soak dried tomatoes in hot water to cover until very soft (about 1 hour).

About 30 minutes before serving, heat oil in a 4- to 5-quart pan over medium heat. Add onion, garlic, carrot, bell pepper, mushrooms, and eggplant; cook, stirring often, until all liquid has evaporated and vegetables are soft (about 20 minutes).

Drain soaked tomatoes, discarding liquid; chop tomatoes and add to eggplant mixture along with peperoncini, pear-shaped tomatoes, zucchini, and olives. Increase heat to high and cook, stirring often, until almost all liquid has evaporated (8 to 10 minutes). Meanwhile, in a 6- to 8-quart pan, cook spaghetti in 4 quarts boiling water just until tender to bite (10 to 12 minutes); or cook according to package directions. Drain well and place in a warm wide serving bowl.

Season vegetable sauce to taste with salt and pepper; spoon over pasta. If desired, serve with cheese to add to taste. Makes 6 servings.

Per serving: 392 calories (15% fat, 72% carbohydrates, 13% protein), 7 g total fat (1 g saturated fat), 71 g carbohydrates, 13 g protein, 0 mg cholesterol, 290 mg sodium

Sautéed Mizuna & Orecchiette

Preparation time: About 10 minutes

Cooking time: About 15 minutes

Mildly tart mizuna, a feathery-leaved member of the mustard family, is becoming increasingly available in well-stocked supermarkets. Delicious raw in salads, the tender-firm leaves are distinctive in cooked dishes, too—as here, where the gently wilted greens combine with hot pasta and Parmesan cheese.

- 1 **pound mizuna, rinsed and drained**
- 12 **ounces orecchiette (ear-shaped pasta) or medium-size dry pasta shells**
- 2 **tablespoons olive oil**
- ¼ **teaspoon crushed red pepper flakes**
- ½ **cup grated Parmesan cheese**

Trim off and discard bare stem ends and any yellow or bruised leaves from mizuna; then chop leaves coarsely and set aside.

In a 5- to 6-quart pan, cook orecchiette in 3 quarts boiling water just until tender to bite (10 to 12 minutes); or cook according to package directions. When pasta is almost done, heat oil in a 4- to 5-quart pan over high heat. Add mizuna and stir until leaves are wilted (2 to 4 minutes).

Drain pasta well and place in a warm wide serving bowl. Add mizuna; mix lightly, using 2 forks. Sprinkle with red pepper flakes and cheese; mix again. Makes 4 servings.

Per serving: 449 calories (22% fat, 62% carbohydrates, 16% protein), 11 g total fat (3 g saturated fat), 69 g carbohydrates, 18 g protein, 8 mg cholesterol, 219 mg sodium

Linguine with Red & Yellow Tomatoes

Preparation time: About 15 minutes

Cooking time: About 10 minutes

Red and yellow cherry tomatoes, halved and seasoned with hot red pepper and aromatic basil, flavor this colorful summer specialty. To accompany the pasta, serve thickly sliced crusty bread and a salad of mixed greens, shredded zucchini, and avocado slices in an oil-lemon dressing.

- 1 **pound dry linguine**
- 2 **tablespoons olive oil**
- 1 **clove garlic, minced or pressed**
- ¼ **teaspoon crushed red pepper flakes**
- 1 **large onion, finely chopped**
- 3 **cups *each* red and yellow cherry tomatoes (about 2 lbs. *total*), cut into halves lengthwise**
- 2 **cups firmly packed fresh basil leaves or ¼ cup dry basil**

Salt and pepper
¼ **to ½ cup grated Parmesan cheese**

In a 6- to 8-quart pan, cook linguine in 4 quarts boiling water just until tender to bite (7 to 9 minutes); or cook according to package directions. Meanwhile, heat oil in a wide frying pan over high heat. Add garlic, red pepper flakes, and onion; cook, stirring often, until onion is lightly browned (3 to 5 minutes). Add tomatoes and basil; cook, stirring gently, just until tomatoes are hot (about 2 minutes).

Drain pasta well and place in a warm wide serving bowl. Pour tomato mixture over pasta; mix lightly, using 2 forks. Season pasta to taste with salt and pepper; serve with cheese to add to taste. Makes 4 to 6 servings.

Per serving: 468 calories (18% fat, 68% carbohydrates, 14% protein), 9 g total fat (2 g saturated fat), 81 g carbohydrates, 17 g protein, 5 mg cholesterol, 136 mg sodium

Farfalle with Chard, Garlic & Ricotta

Preparation time: About 15 minutes

Cooking time: About 10 minutes

For a hearty meal in a hurry, choose this fresh-tasting and quick-to-fix entrée. Alongside, you might serve sliced tomatoes, whole-grain bread, and a fruity light red wine.

- 1 **bunch chard (about 1¼ lbs.), rinsed and drained**
- 10 **ounces dry farfalle (pasta bow ties)**
- 2 **tablespoons olive oil**
- 1 **medium-size onion, finely chopped**
- 4 **cloves garlic, minced or pressed**
- ¾ **cup water**
- 1½ **cups part-skim ricotta cheese, at room temperature**
  Salt and coarsely ground pepper
  Freshly ground nutmeg
  Grated Parmesan cheese (optional)

Trim off and discard ends of chard stems; then cut off remainder of stems at base of each leaf. Thinly slice stems and leaves crosswise, keeping them in separate piles. Set aside.

In a 5- to 6-quart pan, cook farfalle in 3 quarts boiling water just until tender to bite (8 to 10 minutes); or cook according to package directions.

Meanwhile, heat oil in a wide (at least 12-inch) frying pan over medium-high heat. Add onion and chard stems; cook, stirring often, until onion is soft but not browned (3 to 5 minutes). Add garlic and chard leaves and cook, stirring often, until leaves are bright green (about 3 more minutes). Add the ¾ cup water and bring to a boil. Remove from heat and blend in ricotta cheese; season to taste with salt, pepper, and nutmeg.

Drain pasta well and place in a warm wide serving bowl. Add ricotta mixture; mix lightly, using 2 forks. If desired, serve with Parmesan cheese to add to taste. Makes 4 servings.

Per serving: 486 calories (29% fat, 53% carbohydrates, 18% protein), 15 g total fat (6 g saturated fat), 65 g carbohydrates, 22 g protein, 29 mg cholesterol, 399 mg sodium

Green & Red Lasagne

Preparation time: About 35 minutes

Cooking time: About 1 hour and 20 minutes

This meatless lasagne is extra convenient, since you don't precook the pasta; layered with a rich vegetable sauce, it cooks as the casserole bakes.

> **Tomato-Mushroom Sauce (recipe follows)**
> 1 **egg**
> 1 **egg white (about 2 tablespoons)**
> 1 **package (about 10 oz.) frozen chopped spinach, thawed and squeezed dry**
> 2 **cups lowfat cottage cheese**
> ⅓ **cup grated Romano cheese**
> ¼ **teaspoon pepper**
> ⅛ **teaspoon ground nutmeg**
> 8 **ounces dry lasagne noodles**
> 1½ **cups (about 6 oz.) shredded part-skim mozzarella cheese**

Prepare Tomato-Mushroom Sauce. Meanwhile, in a medium-size bowl, beat egg and egg white to blend; then stir in spinach, cottage and Romano cheeses, pepper, and nutmeg.

Spread a fourth of the sauce in a 9- by 13-inch casserole; top with a third of the uncooked lasagne noodles. Spoon on a third of the spinach mixture. Repeat layers of sauce, lasagne, and spinach mixture until all ingredients are used; end with sauce. Sprinkle with mozzarella cheese. Cover tightly with foil. (At this point, you may refrigerate until next day.)

Bake, covered, in a 375° oven until lasagne noodles are tender to bite (about 1 hour; about 1½ hours if refrigerated). Let stand, covered, for about 10 minutes; then cut into squares to serve. Makes 6 to 8 servings.

■ *Tomato-Mushroom Sauce.* Heat 1 teaspoon **olive oil** in a wide (at least 12-inch) nonstick frying pan over medium heat. Add 2 large **onions,** finely chopped; 1 large **red bell pepper** (8 to 10 oz.), seeded and finely chopped; 8 ounces **mushrooms,** thinly sliced; 3 cloves **garlic,** minced or pressed; 1 teaspoon **dry oregano;** and 2½ teaspoons **dry basil.** Cook, stirring often, until liquid has evaporated and onion is very soft (15 to 20 minutes). Stir in 1 large can (about 15 oz.) **tomato sauce,** 1 can (about 6 oz.) **tomato paste,** 1 tablespoon **soy sauce,** and ½ cup **dry red wine.** Cook, stirring, until sauce comes to a boil; use hot.

Per serving: 360 calories (21% fat, 51% carbohydrates, 28% protein), 8 g total fat (3 g saturated fat), 45 g carbohydrates, 25 g protein, 51 mg cholesterol, 1,181 mg sodium

Baked Penne with Radicchio

Preparation time: About 15 minutes

Cooking time: 25 to 35 minutes

Typically served crisp and raw in salads, radicchio takes on a different character when cooked. Here, its bittersweet flavor contrasts nicely with mild pasta, fresh mushrooms, and a touch of Gorgonzola cheese.

> 8 **ounces dry penne or mostaccioli**
> 1 **tablespoon olive oil**
> 8 **ounces mushrooms, sliced**
> 2 **cloves garlic, minced or pressed**
> 1 **teaspoon dry sage**
> 4 **cups lightly packed shredded radicchio**
> ¼ **cup grated Parmesan cheese**
> ¼ **cup crumbled Gorgonzola or other blue-veined cheese**
> **Freshly ground pepper**
> 1 **cup evaporated skim milk**

In a 5- to 6-quart pan, cook penne in 3 quarts boiling water just until almost tender to bite (10 to 12 minutes); or cook a little less than time specified in package directions.

Meanwhile, heat oil in a wide nonstick frying pan over medium heat; add mushrooms, garlic, and sage. Cook, stirring often, until mushrooms are soft and liquid has evaporated (about 10 minutes). Stir in radicchio, then remove pan from heat.

Drain pasta well; add to mushroom mixture along with Parmesan and Gorgonzola cheeses, then mix lightly. Season to taste with pepper. Transfer to a greased 2- to 2½-quart casserole; drizzle evenly with milk. Cover and bake in a 450° oven until bubbly and heated through (15 to 20 minutes). Makes 4 servings.

Per serving: 366 calories (21% fat, 60% carbohydrates, 19% protein), 9 g total fat (2 g saturated fat), 55 g carbohydrates, 17 g protein, 14 mg cholesterol, 263 mg sodium

Created with lowfat dining in mind, hearty Green & Red Lasagne
(recipe on facing page) still offers plenty of satisfying traditional flavor.
Making the casserole is easier than you might expect—just layer uncooked
lasagne noodles with a rich red tomato sauce and a spinach–cottage cheese
filling, then bake. The pasta cooks to tenderness in the oven.

Garden Patch Rigatoni

Preparation time: About 20 minutes

Cooking time: About 50 minutes

This colorful casserole combines vegetables and plump tubular pasta in a savory Cheddar sauce.

- 2 tablespoons margarine
- ½ cup thinly sliced celery
- 2 tablespoons all-purpose flour
- 2 cups nonfat milk
- ½ cup *each* lowfat cottage cheese and shredded sharp Cheddar cheese
- 1 tablespoon Dijon mustard
- ½ teaspoon liquid hot pepper seasoning
- ⅛ teaspoon ground nutmeg
- 8 ounces dry rigatoni or other pasta tubes
- 3 medium-size carrots (about 9 oz. *total*), cut into thin, slanting slices
- 2 cups broccoli flowerets
- 1 cup fresh or frozen corn kernels
- 2 medium-size pear-shaped (Roma-type) tomatoes (5 oz. *total*), seeded and chopped
- ½ cup shredded lowfat Swiss cheese
- 2 tablespoons grated Parmesan cheese

Melt margarine in a 2-quart pan over medium heat; add celery and cook, stirring often, until soft but not browned (about 5 minutes). Add flour and cook, stirring, until bubbly. Remove from heat and gradually stir in milk; return to heat and continue to cook, stirring, until sauce comes to a boil (about 6 minutes). Add cottage and Cheddar cheeses, mustard, hot pepper seasoning, and nutmeg; stir until Cheddar cheese is melted. Remove from heat.

In a 5- to 6-quart pan, cook rigatoni in 3 quarts boiling water just until almost tender to bite (10 to 12 minutes); or cook a little less than time specified in package directions. After pasta has cooked for 5 minutes, add carrots to pan; after 3 more minutes, add broccoli. Drain pasta and vegetables well; pour into a large bowl. Mix in cheese sauce, corn, and tomatoes.

Spread pasta mixture in a greased 2- to 2½-quart casserole; sprinkle with Swiss and Parmesan cheeses. Bake in a 400° oven until lightly browned on top (about 25 minutes). Makes 4 to 6 servings.

Per serving: 437 calories (26% fat, 53% carbohydrates, 21% protein), 13 g total fat (5 g saturated fat), 58 g carbohydrates, 24 g protein, 24 mg cholesterol, 476 mg sodium

Black Beans with Vegetables

Preparation time: About 30 minutes, plus 1 hour to soak beans

Cooking time: About 3 hours

Black beans mingle with brown rice, bell peppers, and chiles in this hearty, nourishing soup-stew.

- 1 pound dried black beans
- 2 tablespoons olive oil or salad oil
- 2 large red onions (about 1½ lbs. *total*), finely chopped
- 2 *each* large green and red bell peppers (2 to 2½ lbs. *total*), seeded and chopped
- 1 small can (about 4 oz.) diced green chiles
- 1 large head garlic (about 2½ oz.), separated into cloves, then minced or pressed
- 1½ tablespoons dry oregano
- 3 vegetable bouillon cubes
- ¼ cup dry sherry (optional)
  Salt and pepper
- 4 to 6 cups hot cooked brown rice

Rinse and sort beans, discarding any debris; drain. In a 6- to 8-quart pan, bring beans and 2 quarts water to a boil; boil for 5 minutes. Cover; remove from heat. Let stand for 1 hour. Drain; set aside.

In same pan, heat oil over medium-high heat. Add onions, bell peppers, chiles, garlic, and oregano. Cook, stirring often, until vegetables are soft and tinged with brown (25 to 30 minutes).

Add beans, 6 cups water, and bouillon cubes to pan. Bring to a boil; reduce heat, cover, and simmer until beans are soft to bite (about 2½ hours), adding more water as needed to keep beans from drying out. Mash some of the beans to thicken mixture slightly. Stir in sherry, if desired. Season to taste with salt and pepper. Mound rice in 8 to 10 wide, shallow bowls; spoon bean mixture over rice. Makes 8 to 10 servings.

Per serving: 375 calories (13% fat, 71% carbohydrates, 16% protein), 5 g total fat (1 g saturated fat), 68 g carbohydrates, 16 g protein, 0 mg cholesterol, 397 mg sodium

Garlic-braised Eggplant & White Beans

Preparation time: About 15 minutes

Cooking time: About 40 minutes

Spoon this bold eggplant-vegetable stew over pasta shells; serve a green salad and bread alongside.

- 1 **small eggplant (about 12 oz.), unpeeled, cut into ½-inch cubes**
- 6 **cloves garlic, thinly sliced**
  Olive oil cooking spray
- 2 **tablespoons olive oil**
- ½ **teaspoon fennel seeds**
- ⅛ **to ¼ teaspoon crushed red pepper flakes**
- 1 **teaspoon Italian herb seasoning or ¼ teaspoon *each* dry basil, dry marjoram, dry oregano, and dry thyme**
- 2 **medium-size onions, thinly sliced**
- 1 **can (about 14½ oz.) pear-shaped tomatoes**
- 1 **can (about 15 oz.) cannellini (white kidney beans), drained and rinsed**
- 8 **ounces medium-size dry pasta shells**
- ½ **cup chopped Italian parsley**
  Salt and freshly ground pepper
  Grated Parmesan cheese (optional)

Spread eggplant cubes in a greased shallow rimmed baking pan; sprinkle with garlic, then spray with cooking spray. Bake in a 425° oven until golden brown (about 20 minutes).

Meanwhile, heat oil in a wide frying pan over medium heat. Add fennel seeds, red pepper flakes, herb seasoning, and onions; cook, stirring often, until onions are soft but not browned (6 to 8 minutes).

Cut up tomatoes; then add tomatoes and their liquid to onion mixture. Stir in baked eggplant. Reduce heat, cover, and simmer for 15 minutes. Stir in cannellini, cover, and continue to simmer until beans are heated through (about 3 more minutes).

While eggplant mixture is simmering, in a 5- to 6-quart pan, cook pasta in 3 quarts boiling water just until tender to bite (10 to 12 minutes); or cook according to package directions. Drain well and divide among 4 to 6 wide, shallow bowls. Stir parsley into eggplant mixture; season to taste with salt and pepper, then spoon over pasta. If desired, serve with cheese to add to taste. Makes 4 to 6 servings.

Per serving: 334 calories (19% fat, 66% carbohydrates, 15% protein), 7 g total fat (1 g saturated fat), 56 g carbohydrates, 13 g protein, 0 mg cholesterol, 267 mg sodium

Garbanzo Curry

Preparation time: About 20 minutes

Cooking time: 40 to 50 minutes

Served over rice, this spicy combination of garbanzo beans and thin-skinned potato chunks is a full meal.

- 2 **tablespoons olive oil or salad oil**
- 1 **large yellow onion, finely chopped**
- 5 **or 6 stalks celery, finely chopped**
- 1 **large red or green bell pepper (8 to 10 oz.), seeded and coarsely chopped**
- 4 **cloves garlic, minced or pressed**
- 1¼ **to 1½ pounds medium-size red thin-skinned potatoes, scrubbed**
- 4 **vegetable bouillon cubes**
- 3½ **cups water**
- 2 **cans (about 15 oz. *each*) garbanzo beans, drained and rinsed**
- 1 **can (about 6 oz.) tomato paste**
- 1 **tablespoon curry powder**
- ¼ **teaspoon ground red pepper (cayenne)**
- 3 **cups hot cooked rice**
  Thinly sliced green onions

Heat oil in a 5- to 6-quart pan over medium heat. Add yellow onion, celery, bell pepper, and garlic. Cook, stirring occasionally, until vegetables are soft but not browned (about 7 minutes). Meanwhile, cut unpeeled potatoes into 1-inch chunks.

To pan, add potatoes, bouillon cubes, water, garbanzos, tomato paste, curry powder, and red pepper; mix well. Bring to a boil over high heat; then reduce heat to medium, cover, and cook until potatoes are tender when pierced (30 to 40 minutes).

Spoon rice in a ring on a warm rimmed platter; mound garbanzo mixture in center. Sprinkle with green onions. Makes 6 servings.

Per serving: 411 calories (17% fat, 71% carbohydrates, 12% protein), 8 g total fat (1 g saturated fat), 74 g carbohydrates, 12 g protein, 0 mg cholesterol, 1,039 mg sodium

*A smart choice for a quick supper, smoky-flavored Pinto
Bean Cakes with Salsa (recipe on facing page) are cornmeal-coated for
crunch. Whip up the nippy topping from your own garden vegetables and
herbs, or use a favorite commercial salsa.*

Pinto Bean Cakes with Salsa

Preparation time: About 15 minutes

Cooking time: About 15 minutes

Dollop a favorite prepared salsa—or your own fresh, homemade sauce—over these cornmeal-coated, cumin-seasoned bean cakes.

1½ **tablespoons salad oil**
1 **small onion, finely chopped**
¼ **cup finely chopped red bell pepper**
2 **cloves garlic, minced or pressed**
1 **medium-size fresh jalapeño chile, seeded and finely chopped**
2 **cans (about 15 oz.** *each***) pinto beans, drained and rinsed**
⅛ **teaspoon liquid smoke**
¼ **cup chopped cilantro**
½ **teaspoon ground cumin**
¼ **teaspoon pepper**
⅓ **cup yellow cornmeal**
Vegetable oil cooking spray (if needed)
½ **to 1 cup purchased or homemade salsa**

Heat 1½ teaspoons of the oil in a wide nonstick frying pan over medium heat. Add onion, bell pepper, garlic, and chile; cook, stirring often, until onion is soft but not browned (about 5 minutes). Meanwhile, place beans in a large bowl and mash coarsely with a potato masher (mashed beans should stick together). Stir in onion mixture; then add liquid smoke, cilantro, cumin, and pepper. Mix well. If necessary, refrigerate until cool.

Spread cornmeal on a sheet of wax paper. Divide bean mixture into 8 equal portions; shape each into a ½-inch-thick cake. Coat cakes with cornmeal.

In pan used to cook onion, heat remaining 1 tablespoon oil over medium-high heat. Add bean cakes and cook, turning once, until golden brown on both sides (8 to 10 minutes); if necessary, spray pan with cooking spray to prevent sticking. Serve with salsa to add to taste. Makes 4 servings (2 cakes *each*).

Per serving: 209 calories (26% fat, 57% carbohydrates, 17% protein), 6 g total fat (1 g saturated fat), 30 g carbohydrates, 9 g protein, 0 mg cholesterol, 615 mg sodium

Curried Hummus with Baked Potatoes

Preparation time: About 10 minutes

Cooking time: About 1 hour

Here's an easy all-vegetable entrée: plump baked potatoes embellished with a quickly assembled hot purée of garbanzos, garlic, curry, and cumin.

4 **very large russet potatoes (2¾ to 3 lbs.** *total***), scrubbed**
1 **vegetable bouillon cube dissolved in ¾ cup hot water**
1 **can (about 15 oz.) garbanzo beans, drained and rinsed**
3 **tablespoons lemon juice**
2 **cloves garlic**
2 **teaspoons curry powder**
½ **teaspoon cumin seeds**
Finely slivered green onions
Salt and pepper

Pierce each unpeeled potato in several places with a fork. Bake in a 350° oven until tender throughout when pierced (about 1 hour).

Meanwhile, in a blender or food processor, combine bouillon mixture, garbanzos, lemon juice, garlic, curry powder, and cumin seeds; whirl until smooth. Transfer purée to a 2-quart pan; cook over medium-high heat, stirring, until reduced to 1½ cups (8 to 10 minutes). Cover and keep warm over lowest heat. (At this point, you may cover and let stand at room temperature for up to 2 hours; reheat before serving, thinning with a little hot water if necessary.)

Make a deep cut lengthwise down center of each potato, then another cut across center. Grasp each potato between cuts and press firmly to split top of potato wide open. Spoon some of the garbanzo purée into center of each potato; pour remainder into a serving bowl. Garnish potatoes with onions; season to taste with salt, pepper, and remaining garbanzo purée. Makes 4 servings.

Per serving: 342 calories (7% fat, 81% carbohydrates, 12% protein), 3 g total fat (0.1 g saturated fat), 70 g carbohydrates, 10 g protein, 0 mg cholesterol, 376 mg sodium

Barley, Lentil & Eggplant Casserole

Preparation time: About 15 minutes

Cooking time: About 1 hour

Combining legumes with grain yields complete protein, just as high in quality as that derived from meat or other animal sources. Here, lentils and barley mingle with browned eggplant in a satisfying main dish to serve with steamed carrots or a leafy green vegetable such as spinach or chard.

    Olive oil cooking spray

2 medium-size eggplants (about 2 lbs. *total*), unpeeled, cut into ¾-inch cubes

5 cups water

5 vegetable bouillon cubes

¾ cup lentils, rinsed and drained

¾ cup pearl barley, rinsed and drained

1 tablespoon dry oregano

1 cup thinly sliced green onions

⅓ cup chopped fresh mint or 3 tablespoons dry mint

2 tablespoons olive oil

1 teaspoon pepper

1½ cups (about 6 oz.) shredded part-skim mozzarella cheese

    Mint sprigs

Spray 2 shallow rimmed baking pans with cooking spray. Spread eggplant cubes evenly in pans; spray with cooking spray. Bake eggplant in a 425° oven, turning with a spatula several times, until well browned and soft when pressed (30 to 35 minutes).

Meanwhile, in a 3- to 4-quart pan, bring 5 cups water to a boil; add bouillon cubes and stir until dissolved. Add lentils, barley, and oregano. Reduce heat, cover, and simmer until lentils and barley are tender to bite (about 25 minutes). Drain, reserving liquid.

Lightly mix eggplant, lentil-barley mixture, onions, chopped mint, oil, pepper, 1 cup of the cheese, and 1 cup of the reserved lentil-barley liquid. Spread in a 9- by 13-inch casserole; sprinkle with remaining ½ cup cheese. (At this point, you may cover and refrigerate until next day.)

Cover and bake in a 425° oven until heated through (about 30 minutes; about 45 minutes if refrigerated). Garnish with mint sprigs. Makes 6 servings.

Per serving: 338 calories (27% fat, 52% carbohydrates, 21% protein), 11 g total fat (4 g saturated fat), 46 g carbohydrates, 19 g protein, 16 mg cholesterol, 910 mg sodium

Broccoli with Spiced Rice & Pine Nuts

Preparation time: About 5 minutes

Cooking time: About 30 minutes

Golden raisins and chili powder add interest to an appealing medley of white rice and tender broccoli. (For a delicious broccoli-rice side dish, try Winter Flower Bud Rice, page 80.)

¼ cup pine nuts or slivered almonds

2 teaspoons olive oil or salad oil

⅔ cup long-grain white rice

⅓ cup golden raisins

2 teaspoons chili powder

2 vegetable bouillon cubes dissolved in 2½ cups hot water

1¼ pounds broccoli

Toast pine nuts in a wide nonstick frying pan over medium-low heat until lightly browned (about 3 minutes), stirring. Remove from pan and set aside.

In same pan, heat oil over medium-high heat. Add rice, raisins, and chili powder. Cook, stirring, until rice begins to turn opaque (about 3 minutes). Stir in bouillon mixture; reduce heat, cover tightly, and simmer for 15 minutes.

Meanwhile, cut off and discard tough ends of broccoli stalks. Cut off flowerets in bite-size pieces and set aside. Thinly slice remainder of stalks.

Distribute broccoli flowerets and sliced stalks over rice mixture. Cover and continue to cook until broccoli is just tender to bite (7 to 10 more minutes). Mix gently, transfer to a warm platter, and sprinkle with pine nuts. Makes 4 servings.

Per serving: 247 calories (26% fat, 62% carbohydrates, 12% protein), 8 g total fat (1 g saturated fat), 41 g carbohydrates, 8 g protein, 0 mg cholesterol, 499 mg sodium

■ Pictured on page 62

Wild Spanish Rice

Preparation time: About 15 minutes

Cooking time: About 1¾ hours

Elegant wild rice is balanced by nutty-tasting brown rice in this tomato-sauced, olive-strewn casserole.

- ½ cup wild rice
- 2 vegetable bouillon cubes dissolved in 2 cups hot water
- 1 tablespoon olive oil or salad oil
- 1 medium-size red onion, thinly sliced
- 2 cloves garlic, minced or pressed
- 1 cup long-grain brown rice
- 1 teaspoon chili powder
- 2½ cups tomato juice
- 1 medium-size green bell pepper (about 6 oz.), seeded and chopped
- 2 large pear-shaped (Roma-type) tomatoes (about 6 oz. *total*), seeded and chopped
- ½ cup pimento-stuffed green olives, cut into halves lengthwise
- ¼ cup dry-roasted peanuts

Place wild rice in a fine wire strainer and rinse under running water. In a wide nonstick frying pan, bring bouillon mixture to a boil over high heat. Add wild rice, reduce heat, cover tightly, and simmer until rice is tender to bite (about 45 minutes). Drain, reserving broth; set rice and broth aside.

In same pan, heat oil over medium heat. Add onion and garlic; cook, stirring often, until onion is soft and golden (6 to 8 minutes). Add brown rice, increase heat to medium-high, and cook, stirring, until rice begins to turn opaque (about 3 minutes). Add chili powder, tomato juice, and reserved broth. Reduce heat, cover tightly, and simmer until rice is tender to bite (45 to 50 minutes). Add wild rice, bell pepper, tomatoes, and olives; stir gently until heated through (about 2 minutes). Transfer to a warm serving dish and sprinkle with peanuts. Makes 4 to 6 servings.

Per serving: 319 calories (26% fat, 63% carbohydrates, 11% protein), 10 g total fat (1 g saturated fat), 52 g carbohydrates, 9 g protein, 0 mg cholesterol, 1,147 mg sodium

Pineapple, Strawberry & Apple Salad

Preparation time: About 25 minutes

A trio of fresh fruits, dressed with yogurt and served with cottage cheese, makes a handsome salad to enjoy with bran muffins for a light warm-weather supper.

- 1 medium-size pineapple (about 3 lbs.)
- 1 small tart green apple
- 1 cup coarsely chopped strawberries
- ⅓ cup plain lowfat yogurt
- 8 to 16 butter lettuce leaves, rinsed and crisped
- 8 whole strawberries
- 1 cup small-curd cottage cheese

Cut peel and eyes from pineapple. Slice off top third of pineapple; cut out and discard core, then chop fruit. Place chopped pineapple in a medium-size bowl and set aside. Cut remaining pineapple lengthwise into 8 wedges; cut off and discard core from each wedge.

Core apple and cut into ½-inch pieces. Add apple, chopped strawberries, and yogurt to chopped pineapple; mix lightly. (At this point, you may cover and re-frigerate fruit mixture and pineapple wedges separately for up to 4 hours.)

On each of 8 salad plates, arrange 1 or 2 lettuce leaves, a pineapple wedge, a whole strawberry, a dollop of cottage cheese, and an eighth of the chopped fruit mixture. Makes 8 servings.

Per serving: 92 calories (17% fat, 66% carbohydrates, 17% protein), 2 g total fat (1 g saturated fat), 16 g carbohydrates, 4 g protein, 4 mg cholesterol, 115 mg sodium

Side Dishes

No matter how simple the entrée, the right accompaniment can make mealtime sparkle. Chosen and cooked with care, side dishes of vegetables, fruits, or grains provide a maximum of appetite appeal (and a bonus of B vitamins and minerals) with a minimum of fat.

From eggplant to turnips, properly cooked vegetables offer surprisingly sweet flavors that present a fine contrast to the other foods on your plate. If you select each variety at its peak, then season skillfully—using freshly ground pepper, other spices, and fresh herbs—you'll have little reason to add fat. Be creative in your vegetable choices, too; experiment with colorful combinations of two or more kinds. And don't forget old favorites. Potatoes, for example, are both light and lean if cooked with little or no added fat; they're a perfect partner for most protein foods, as well as an excellent source of complex carbohydrates and vitamin C.

Fruits have long been popular accompaniments for meats and poultry. To bring color and variety to your lowfat cooking, go beyond such familiar choices as applesauce and cranberry jelly; try grilling or broiling pineapple, papaya, or apple wedges, or achieve more piquant results by stirring up a salsa of diced fruit accented with minced fresh chiles.

Finally, versatile grains such as rice (long- or short-grain, brown or white) and pasta in its many eye-pleasing shapes also bring welcome warmth to lean meals.

While a lemon- and herb-stuffed chicken roasts, stir
together luscious Winter Flower Bud Rice (recipe on page 80). This
fresh, easy risotto combines rice and two robust winter
vegetables—broccoli and cauliflower—in one irresistible dish.

Potato Risotto

Preparation time: About 10 minutes

Cooking time: About 35 minutes

This rich-tasting dish has the creamy texture of the famous Italian rice specialty—but it's made with shredded potatoes, cooked gently in chicken broth and finished with evaporated skim milk and a touch of Parmesan cheese. Serve it with sizzling grilled chicken breasts or veal chops.

> 1 tablespoon margarine
> 1 small onion, finely chopped
> ½ teaspoon minced fresh thyme or
>   ¼ teaspoon dry thyme
> 1 clove garlic, minced or pressed
> 1¾ cups low-sodium chicken broth
> 3 medium-size thin-skinned potatoes
>   (about 1¼ lbs. *total*)
> ¼ cup *each* evaporated skim milk and
>   grated Parmesan cheese
>   Freshly ground nutmeg
>   Thyme sprigs (optional)

Melt margarine in a 2- to 3-quart pan over medium heat. Add onion and minced thyme; cook, stirring often, until onion is soft but not browned (3 to 5 minutes). Stir in garlic, then add broth. Increase heat to high and bring mixture to a boil; boil until reduced to 1½ cups (about 3 minutes).

Peel and shred potatoes. Add to onion mixture; reduce heat to medium-low and cook, uncovered, stirring often, until potatoes are tender to bite (about 25 minutes). Remove from heat and mix in milk and cheese. Season to taste with nutmeg. Spoon into a warm serving bowl; garnish with thyme sprigs, if desired. Makes 4 to 6 servings.

Per serving: 145 calories (26% fat, 58% carbohydrates, 16% protein), 4 g total fat (1 g saturated fat), 21 g carbohydrates, 6 g protein, 4 mg cholesterol, 469 mg sodium

Garlic Potatoes

Preparation time: About 10 minutes

Baking time: 45 minutes to 1 hour

Simple to prepare, these crusty, pungently flavored potatoes are good with hearty stews such as Hunter's-style Lamb Stew (page 44). You might also serve them with sandwiches, as a pleasant change from French fries; try them with Turkey & Mushroom Burgers (page 52), for example.

>   Olive oil cooking spray
> 2½ to 3 pounds small red thin-skinned
>   potatoes (*each* 1½ to 2 inches in diameter),
>   scrubbed and quartered lengthwise
> 6 cloves garlic, quartered lengthwise
>   Paprika
>   Salt and freshly ground pepper

Spray a shallow rimmed baking pan with cooking spray. Place potatoes and garlic in pan and stir to mix; spray with cooking spray. Sprinkle with paprika. Bake in a 425° oven until potatoes are golden brown and tender when pierced (45 minutes to 1 hour). Season to taste with salt and pepper. Makes 8 servings.

Per serving: 130 calories (3% fat, 88% carbohydrates, 9% protein), 0.4 g total fat (0 g saturated fat), 29 g carbohydrates, 3 g protein, 0 mg cholesterol, 12 mg sodium

Mashed Potatoes & Turnips with Garlic

Preparation time: About 15 minutes

Cooking time: 45 to 50 minutes

Earthy-flavored potatoes and turnips, mashed until smooth and blended with sweet roasted garlic and onion, make a pleasing side dish for grilled or roasted meat or chicken.

> 1 tablespoon olive oil
> 1 large onion, finely chopped
> 3 large heads garlic (about 9 oz. *total*)
> 1¼ pounds turnips
> 1½ pounds large russet potatoes
> 1¾ cups low-sodium chicken broth
> ¼ cup evaporated skim milk
> Salt and ground white pepper

Drizzle oil into a shallow rimmed baking pan. Add onion and mix to coat with oil; then push onion to one side. Cut unpeeled garlic heads into halves crosswise; place, cut sides down, in pan with onion. Bake in a 375° oven, stirring onions occasionally, until onions are browned and garlic is very tender when pierced in center (40 to 45 minutes). Set aside until garlic is cool enough to touch.

While vegetables are baking, peel and quarter turnips and potatoes. In a 3- to 4-quart pan, combine turnips, potatoes, and broth; bring to a boil over high heat. Reduce heat, cover, and boil gently until vegetables are very tender when pierced and almost all broth has been absorbed (about 25 minutes).

Squeeze garlic from skins into a small bowl; discard skins. Using the back of a spoon, mash garlic to a smooth paste. Mix in browned onions, then set mixture aside.

Transfer potato mixture to a large bowl. Using an electric mixer or a potato masher, beat until smooth. Add milk and garlic-onion mixture; beat until smooth and creamy. Season to taste with salt and white pepper, then transfer to a shallow 1½- to 2-quart casserole. Broil about 4 inches below heat until top is dappled with golden brown (3 to 5 minutes). Makes 6 servings.

Per serving: 204 calories (14% fat, 73% carbohydrates, 13% protein), 3 g total fat (0.5 g saturated fat), 39 g carbohydrates, 7 g protein, 0.4 mg cholesterol, 94 mg sodium

Brussels Sprouts with Mustard Glaze

Preparation time: About 10 minutes

Cooking time: About 10 minutes

To tempt both the eye and the palate, accompany a simply cooked main dish—such as broiled chops or chicken breasts—with steamed whole Brussels sprouts in a shiny mustard and brown sugar glaze.

> 4 cups Brussels sprouts (about 1¼ lbs.)
> 3 tablespoons firmly packed brown sugar
> 2 tablespoons cider vinegar
> 1 tablespoon Dijon mustard
> 2 teaspoons margarine
> Salt

Discard coarse outer leaves from Brussels sprouts. Then rinse sprouts, drain, and place on a rack above 1 inch of boiling water in a large pan. Cover pan and steam sprouts over high heat until tender when pierced (about 10 minutes).

When sprouts are almost done, combine sugar, vinegar, mustard, and margarine in a wide nonstick frying pan. Cook over medium-high heat, stirring, until mixture bubbles vigorously. Stir in sprouts; season to taste with salt. Makes 4 servings.

Per serving: 116 calories (18% fat, 69% carbohydrates, 13% protein), 3 g total fat (0.4 g saturated fat), 22 g carbohydrates, 4 g protein, 0 mg cholesterol, 170 mg sodium

Grilling lean lamb chops tonight? Simply Perfect Eggplant (recipe on facing page) is a tempting complement. The recipe features petite Oriental eggplant, baked with only a whisper of olive oil and topped with an herb-seasoned vegetable blend. You might also serve a bowl of fresh green peas.

■ *Pictured on facing page*

Simply Perfect Eggplant

Preparation time: About 20 minutes

Cooking time: About 25 minutes

Slices of slender, delicate-flavored Oriental eggplant bake to tenderness with very little added oil—in fact, you can simply use an olive oil cooking spray. Finish the sweet-tasting slices with a colorful topping of dried tomatoes, red bell pepper, and mushrooms.

> Olive oil cooking spray
>
> 6 Oriental eggplants (1 to 1½ lbs. *total*)
>
> ¼ cup dried tomatoes
>
> 2 teaspoons olive oil
>
> 1 small onion, finely chopped
>
> 8 ounces mushrooms, finely chopped
>
> 1 small red bell pepper (about 5 oz.), seeded and chopped
>
> ½ teaspoon *each* dry oregano and dry marjoram
>
> 2 cloves garlic, minced or pressed
>
> Salt and pepper
>
> Chopped parsley

Spray a shallow rimmed baking pan with cooking spray. Cut eggplants crosswise into ½-inch-thick slices; arrange in a single layer in pan. Spray with cooking spray. Bake in a 425° oven until well browned and very soft when pressed (about 25 minutes).

Meanwhile, soak tomatoes in boiling water to cover until soft (about 15 minutes). Drain, discarding liquid; finely chop tomatoes.

Heat oil in a wide nonstick frying pan over medium heat. Add tomatoes, onion, mushrooms, bell pepper, oregano, marjoram, and garlic. Cook, stirring often, until mushrooms are lightly browned but mixture is still moist (10 to 15 minutes). Season to taste with salt and pepper.

To serve, transfer eggplant slices to a warm platter; top with mushroom mixture and sprinkle with parsley. Makes 4 to 6 servings.

Per serving: 82 calories (27% fat, 60% carbohydrates, 13% protein), 3 g total fat (0.3 g saturated fat), 14 g carbohydrates, 3 g protein, 0 mg cholesterol, 12 mg sodium

Broiled Pineapple with Basil

Preparation time: About 10 minutes

Broiling time: 3 to 4 minutes

Hot pineapple drizzled with honey and vinegar has a tart-sweet flavor that perfectly complements teriyaki-seasoned poultry, lamb, or pork.

> ¼ cup honey
>
> 2 tablespoons cider vinegar
>
> 1 tablespoon finely chopped crystallized ginger
>
> 1 teaspoon dry basil
>
> 1 medium-size pineapple (about 3 lbs.), peeled and cored
>
> Basil sprigs (optional)

In a small pan, combine honey, vinegar, ginger, and dry basil. Stir over low heat until warm (about 3 minutes); set aside.

Cut pineapple crosswise into ½-inch-thick slices; or cut lengthwise into ½-inch-thick wedges. Arrange pineapple pieces in a single layer in a shallow rimmed baking pan; drizzle with honey mixture. Broil about 4 inches below heat until pineapple is lightly browned (3 to 4 minutes). Using a wide spatula, transfer pineapple to a warm platter or plates. Spoon pan juices over pineapple and garnish with basil sprigs, if desired. Makes 4 to 6 servings.

Per serving: 133 calories (4% fat, 94% carbohydrates, 2% protein), 1 g total fat (0 g saturated fat), 35 g carbohydrates, 1 g protein, 0 mg cholesterol, 4 mg sodium

■ *Pictured on page 75*

Winter Flower Bud Rice

Preparation time: About 10 minutes

Cooking time: About 35 minutes

When cauliflower and broccoli are at their seasonal peak, try this savory, vegetable-studded rice as a companion to your favorite veal and poultry entrées.

> 2 **cups cauliflower flowerets**
> 2 **cups broccoli flowerets**
> 1 **tablespoon margarine**
> 1 **large onion, finely chopped**
> 2 **cloves garlic, minced or pressed**
> 1 **cup short-grain rice, such as pearl rice**
> ½ **cup dry white wine**
> 3 **to 3¼ cups low-sodium chicken broth**
> ⅔ **cup grated Parmesan cheese**
> **Freshly ground pepper**

In a 3- to 4-quart pan, bring 2 quarts water to a boil. Add cauliflower and cook for 3 minutes; add broccoli and continue to cook until both vegetables are barely tender when pierced (about 2 more minutes). Drain, immerse in ice water until cool, and drain again.

Melt margarine in a wide nonstick frying pan over medium heat. Add onion and garlic. Cook, stirring often, until onion begins to brown (about 5 minutes). Add rice and cook, stirring often, until rice begins to turn opaque (about 3 minutes). Mix in wine and 3 cups of the broth; cook, stirring, until mixture comes to a boil. Reduce heat so mixture boils gently; continue to cook, stirring occasionally, for 10 more minutes.

Stir cauliflower and broccoli into rice mixture. Continue to cook until rice is just tender to bite and almost all broth has been absorbed (8 to 10 more minutes). Add more broth if rice becomes too dry. Stir in ⅓ cup of the cheese; season to taste with pepper. Spoon into a warm serving bowl; sprinkle with remaining ⅓ cup cheese. Makes 6 servings.

Per serving: 241 calories (23% fat, 60% carbohydrates, 17% protein), 6 g total fat (2 g saturated fat), 35 g carbohydrates, 10 g protein, 7 mg cholesterol, 237 mg sodium

Golden Curried Couscous

Preparation time: About 15 minutes

Cooking time: 5 to 10 minutes

Studded with raisins, sprinkled with pistachios, and spiced with ginger and curry powder, this fluffy couscous is delightful with pork, chicken, or lamb.

> 2¼ **cups low-sodium chicken broth**
> ¾ **cup golden raisins**
> 6 **tablespoons lemon juice**
> 3 **tablespoons finely chopped crystallized ginger**
> 1 **tablespoon margarine**
> ¾ **teaspoon curry powder**
> 1½ **cups couscous**
> ½ **cup thinly sliced celery**
> ⅓ **cup thinly sliced green onions**
> 3 **tablespoons chopped cilantro**
> ¼ **cup coarsely chopped salted roasted pistachio nuts**
> **Cilantro sprigs**

In a 2- to 3-quart pan, bring broth to a boil over high heat. Stir in raisins, lemon juice, ginger, margarine, curry powder, and couscous. Cover pan and remove from heat; let stand for 5 to 10 minutes. Fluff couscous with a fork. (At this point, you may cover and refrigerate until next day; bring to room temperature before serving.)

Serve couscous warm or at room temperature. Just before serving, stir in celery, onions, and chopped cilantro. Mound couscous mixture in a serving dish; sprinkle with pistachios and garnish with cilantro sprigs. Makes 6 servings.

Per serving: 321 calories (15% fat, 74% carbohydrates, 11% protein), 6 g total fat (1 g saturated fat), 61 g carbohydrates, 9 g protein, 0 mg cholesterol, 67 mg sodium

Tortellini with Green Cabbage

Preparation time: About 5 minutes

Cooking time: About 15 minutes

Here's a hearty, ultra-simple accompaniment to thinly sliced top round of beef, herbed pork chops, or broiled chicken breasts.

- 3 beef bouillon cubes dissolved in 3 cups hot water
- 1 package (9 oz.) fresh cheese-filled tortellini
- 4 cups finely shredded green cabbage
  Freshly ground pepper
  Light sour cream (optional)

In a wide 3-quart pan, bring bouillon mixture to a boil over high heat. Add tortellini, reduce heat, and boil gently for 10 minutes. Add cabbage and continue to cook gently, stirring occasionally, until pasta has absorbed almost all liquid and is just tender to bite (3 to 4 minutes). Season to taste with pepper. Serve with sour cream to add to taste, if desired. Makes 4 servings.

Per serving: 211 calories (14% fat, 64% carbohydrates, 22% protein), 3 g total fat (0.1 g saturated fat), 34 g carbohydrates, 12 g protein, 35 mg cholesterol, 881 mg sodium

Pasta Risotto with Asparagus

Preparation time: About 5 minutes

Cooking time: About 15 minutes

Simmered in broth and dotted with sliced fresh asparagus, tiny pasta shapes—stars, rice, or letters of the alphabet—make a tempting "risotto" to accompany poultry or fish hot from the grill.

- 3 cups low-sodium chicken broth
- 1 cup (5 to 7 oz.) tiny dry pasta shapes, such as stars, rice, or letters of the alphabet
- 2 cups 1-inch-long pieces of asparagus
- ½ cup grated Parmesan cheese

In a 2- to 3-quart pan, bring broth to a boil over high heat. Add pasta, reduce heat, and boil gently for 8 minutes. Add asparagus and continue to cook, stirring often, until almost all liquid has been absorbed and pasta and asparagus are just tender to bite (5 to 7 more minutes). Stir in ¼ cup of the cheese. Spoon risotto into a warm serving dish; sprinkle with remaining ¼ cup cheese. Makes 4 to 6 servings.

Per serving: 172 calories (20% fat, 57% carbohydrates, 23% protein), 4 g total fat (2 g saturated fat), 24 g carbohydrates, 10 g protein, 6 mg cholesterol, 184 mg sodium

Breads

Long revered as the staff of life, bread is a perfect choice for lowfat life-styles. At its most basic, it's little more than flour mixed with water and (usually) a leavening agent such as yeast or baking powder; depending on taste and custom, it may or may not include salt.

To add fiber to your bread and vary its texture and flavor, venture beyond the familiar all-purpose flour—choose whole wheat flour or multigrain mixtures, such as cornmeal or wheat germ plus a whole-grain flour. Such substitutions won't appreciably increase fat content. (Whole-grain flours do contain a bit more fat than more refined flour, but it's of the desirable unsaturated type—see page 101.)

If you're new to bread baking, quick breads (those leavened with baking powder and/or baking soda) are a good starting point. Our prune tea bread, apricot-nut muffins, and fruit-studded coffeecake go together and bake in minutes; choose them for weekend breakfasts, or serve as an accompaniment to soup or salad.

If you're an experienced baker, you'll want to try our flavorful yeast breads. Italian-style focaccia (with your choice of three toppings) and cleverly shaped rolls offer both superb eating and delicious good looks.

Summer fruits take center stage in a light, pretty brunch to enjoy outdoors on the patio. Savor wedges of Apricot-Blackberry Cornmeal Kuchen (recipe on page 85) with tart, creamy Cantaloupe & Yogurt Shakes (recipe on page 88).

Prune-Buttermilk Bread

Preparation time: About 15 minutes

Baking time: 40 to 45 minutes

This pleasingly moist quick bread is a good partner for your favorite spiced tea. Be sure to use buttermilk that contains no more than one percent milk fat.

    1   cup chopped pitted prunes
    1   cup water
    1   cup whole wheat flour
    1½ cups all-purpose flour
    1½ teaspoons baking powder
    1   teaspoon baking soda
    ¼   cup margarine, at room temperature
    1   cup sugar
    1   egg
    2   teaspoons vanilla
    1   cup lowfat buttermilk

In a small pan, combine prunes and water. Bring to a boil over high heat; reduce heat and boil gently until prunes are plump (about 1 minute). Drain well, reserving ½ cup liquid. Set prunes and liquid aside separately.

In a medium-size bowl, stir together whole wheat flour, all-purpose flour, baking powder, and baking soda until well blended; set aside.

In a large bowl, beat margarine and sugar until well blended. Beat in egg, then vanilla. Stir in a third of the flour mixture; blend in buttermilk. Stir in half the remaining flour mixture; blend in reserved ½ cup prune liquid. Add remaining flour mixture; stir just until dry ingredients are evenly moistened. Blend in prunes. Divide batter between 2 greased 4½- by 8½-inch loaf pans.

Bake in a 350° oven until tops of loaves are well browned and edges pull away from pans (40 to 45 minutes). Let cool in pans on a rack for 15 minutes. Then invert pans and turn out loaves onto rack; let cool completely. To serve, cut loaves into about ½-inch-thick slices. Makes 2 loaves (about 16 slices *each*).

Per slice: 89 calories (18% fat, 75% carbohydrates, 7% protein), 2 g total fat (0.5 g saturated fat), 17 g carbohydrates, 2 g protein, 7 mg cholesterol, 73 mg sodium

Apricot Graham Muffins

Preparation time: About 15 minutes

Baking time: About 20 minutes

Made with crunchy wheat germ and graham or whole wheat flour, these muffins are definitely on the sturdy side. Chopped dried apricots add a lively sweet-tart flavor. (Graham flour is usually somewhat coarser in texture than whole wheat flour.)

    1½ cups graham or whole wheat flour
    ½   cup toasted wheat germ
    ¼   cup granulated sugar
    2   teaspoons baking powder
    1   teaspoon baking soda
    ⅔   cup chopped dried apricots
    ⅓   cup chopped pecans or walnuts
    2   tablespoons salad oil
    1   egg
    1   egg white (about 2 tablespoons)
    1   cup vanilla or plain nonfat yogurt
    3   tablespoons firmly packed brown sugar

In a large bowl, stir together flour, wheat germ, granulated sugar, baking powder, and baking soda until well blended. Stir in apricots and pecans; set mixture aside.

In a medium-size bowl, combine oil, egg, egg white, and yogurt; beat with a whisk until well blended. Add yogurt mixture to flour mixture; stir just until dry ingredients are evenly moistened. Spoon batter into greased 2½-inch muffin pans, filling to pan rims. Sprinkle evenly with brown sugar.

Bake in a 375° oven until edges of muffins are browned and tops spring back when lightly touched (about 20 minutes). Let muffins cool in pans on a rack for 2 to 3 minutes, then remove carefully from pans. Serve warm. Makes 12 muffins.

Per muffin: 163 calories (29% fat, 60% carbohydrates, 11% protein), 6 g total fat (1 g saturated fat), 26 g carbohydrates, 5 g protein, 18 mg cholesterol, 152 mg sodium

■ Pictured on page 83

Apricot-Blackberry Cornmeal Kuchen

Preparation time: About 15 minutes

Baking time: 30 to 35 minutes

Apricots and fresh berries share the spotlight in a luscious coffeecake that's just right for a summertime brunch or weekend breakfast.

> ½ **cup** *each* **all-purpose flour and yellow cornmeal**
>
> 1½ **teaspoons baking powder**
>
> 1 **egg**
>
> ⅓ **cup firmly packed brown sugar**
>
> ½ **cup lowfat buttermilk**
>
> 2 **tablespoons salad oil**
>
> 5 **medium-size apricots (about 12 oz.** *total***), halved and pitted**
>
> 10 **blackberries or boysenberries**
>
> 2 **tablespoons granulated sugar**

In a large bowl, stir together flour, cornmeal, and baking powder until well blended; set aside.

In a medium-size bowl, combine egg, brown sugar, buttermilk, and oil; beat with a whisk until well blended. Add buttermilk mixture to cornmeal mixture and stir just until dry ingredients are evenly moistened.

Spread batter in a greased 8-inch-round baking pan or quiche pan. Gently press apricot halves, pitted sides up, into batter. Place a berry in hollow of each apricot half.

Bake in a 350° oven until center of cake feels firm when lightly touched (30 to 35 minutes). Sprinkle with granulated sugar. Let cool slightly, then cut into wedges and serve warm. Makes 8 servings.

Per serving: 174 calories (24% fat, 69% carbohydrates, 7% protein), 5 g total fat (1 g saturated fat), 30 g carbohydrates, 3 g protein, 27 mg cholesterol, 107 mg sodium

---

■ Pictured on page 35

Southwest Blue Cornbread Sticks

Preparation time: About 20 minutes

Baking time: About 25 minutes

A staple in the Southwest, blue cornmeal is now available in other parts of the country, too; you'll find it in specialty food shops and many well-stocked supermarkets. Though interchangeable with yellow or white cornmeal, it does add its own distinctive parched-corn flavor to tortillas and baked goods—such as these chile-and-cheese cornsticks.

> 1 **cup plus 2 tablespoons blue cornmeal**
>
> 2 **tablespoons salad oil**
>
> 1 **medium-size onion, finely chopped**
>
> 1 **small fresh jalapeño chile, seeded and finely chopped**
>
> 1 **cup all-purpose flour**
>
> 1 **tablespoon** *each* **sugar and baking powder**
>
> 1¼ **cups nonfat milk**
>
> 1 **egg**
>
> ½ **cup shredded part-skim jack cheese**

Use 2 tablespoons of the cornmeal to coat greased cornstick pans or 1½-inch muffin pans; set pans aside.

Heat oil in a medium-size nonstick frying pan over medium heat. Add onion and chile; cook, stirring often, until onion is lightly browned (6 to 8 minutes). Set aside.

In a large bowl, stir together flour, sugar, baking powder, and remaining 1 cup cornmeal until well blended; set aside.

In a medium-size bowl, combine milk and egg; beat with a whisk until well blended. Add milk mixture, cheese, and onion mixture to cornmeal mixture. Stir just until dry ingredients are evenly moistened.

Spoon batter into pans, filling almost to rims. Bake in a 375° oven until cornsticks are lightly browned and feel firm when lightly pressed (about 25 minutes). Let cool in pans on a rack for about 10 minutes, then loosen carefully and remove from pans. Serve warm. Makes 14 cornbread sticks.

Per cornbread stick: 121 calories (25% fat, 61% carbohydrates, 14% protein), 3 g total fat (1 g saturated fat), 18 g carbohydrates, 4 g protein, 18 mg cholesterol, 134 mg sodium

Wood-fired ovens all over Italy yield golden-crusted treasures
with musical names: flatbreads such as schiacciata, focaccia, and piadina.
Focaccia comes from Liguria, the Mediterranean coastal region around
Genoa; our version (recipe on facing page) features your choice of three
toppings (we show two—tomato and green olive).

■ *Pictured on facing page*

Savory Focaccia

Preparation time: About 1 hour, plus about 1½ hours for dough to rise

Baking time: 35 to 45 minutes

Thicker and softer than pizza, focaccia also features leaner toppings—such as baked tomatoes accented with a little olive oil, a dappling of salty olives, or a savory combination of onions and sweet raisins. Serve squares or strips of this distinctive bread as a snack; or offer with a main-dish soup or salad.

1½	**cups warm water (about 110°F)**
1	**package active dry yeast**
½	**teaspoon salt**
2	**tablespoons olive oil**
4	**to 4¼ cups all-purpose flour**
	Tomato Topping, Onion Topping, or Olive Topping (recipes follow)
	Olive oil cooking spray
	Salt and pepper

Pour water into a large bowl; sprinkle with yeast. Let stand for 5 minutes to soften yeast, then stir in salt and oil. Add 2½ cups of the flour; stir to blend. Beat with an electric mixer until dough is elastic and stretchy (3 to 5 minutes). Stir in 1⅓ cups more flour.

To knead with a dough hook, beat until dough is stretchy and cleans sides of bowl (5 to 7 minutes); if dough is sticky, add more flour, about 1 tablespoon at a time.

To knead by hand, scrape dough onto a floured board and knead until smooth and springy (5 to 10 minutes), adding more flour as needed. Place dough in an oiled bowl; turn dough over to oil top.

Cover bowl of dough (kneaded by either method) with plastic wrap. Let dough rise in a warm place until doubled (about 45 minutes). Or, if desired, let rise in refrigerator for up to a day. Shortly before you are ready to shape dough, prepare topping of your choice.

Punch down dough, then knead briefly on a lightly floured board to expel air. Spray a shallow rimmed 10- by 15-inch baking pan with cooking spray. Place dough in pan. Press and stretch dough to fill pan evenly. (If dough is too elastic, let rest for a few minutes, then stretch again; repeat as needed.) Cover pan lightly with plastic wrap and let dough rise in a warm place until doubled (about 45 minutes).

Spray dough with cooking spray. With your fingers, gently press dough down all over, forming dimples in the surface. Evenly cover dough with topping. Sprinkle with herbs specified in topping recipe (if using tomato or olive version); sprinkle lightly with salt and pepper.

Bake in a 400° oven until focaccia is well browned at edges and on bottom (35 to 45 minutes). Let cool for at least 5 minutes, then cut into strips or squares and serve warm or at room temperature. (Or reheat: cover loosely with foil and heat in a 350° oven for 10 to 15 minutes.) Makes 12 servings.

■ *Tomato Topping.* Spray a shallow rimmed 10- by 15-inch baking pan with **olive oil cooking spray.** Cut 2 pounds large **pear-shaped (Roma-type) tomatoes** lengthwise into ½-inch-thick slices. Place slices in pan in a single layer, overlapping slightly if needed. Drizzle with 2 tablespoons **olive oil.** Bake in a 450° oven until tomatoes look dry and pan juices have evaporated (about 30 minutes). Using a wide spatula, gently loosen tomatoes from pan. After arranging tomatoes on risen dough, sprinkle with 1 teaspoon *each* **dry basil** and **dry oregano.**

Per serving with Tomato Topping: 204 calories (24% fat, 66% carbohydrates, 10% protein), 6 g total fat (1 g saturated fat), 34 g carbohydrates, 5 g protein, 0 mg cholesterol, 98 mg sodium

■ *Onion Topping.* Slice 3 medium-size **onions** in half lengthwise, then cut each half into ¼-inch-thick slices. In a shallow rimmed 10- by 15-inch baking pan, mix onions and 2 tablespoons **olive oil.** Bake in a 450° oven, stirring occasionally, until onions are soft but not browned (about 20 minutes). Stir in ¼ cup **golden raisins** and 1 tablespoon drained **minced anchovies.**

Per serving with Onion Topping: 221 calories (23% fat, 67% carbohydrates, 10% protein), 6 g total fat (1 g saturated fat), 37 g carbohydrates, 6 g protein, 6 mg cholesterol, 149 mg sodium

■ *Olive Topping.* Cut 20 to 25 **pitted Spanish-style olives** (*each* at least 1 inch long) into halves lengthwise. Arrange olives, cut sides down, over dough about 1 inch apart. Sprinkle with 1 teaspoon **dry thyme.**

Per serving with Olive Topping: 181 calories (21% fat, 69% carbohydrates, 10% protein), 4 g total fat (0.5 g saturated fat), 31 g carbohydrates, 4 g protein, 0 mg cholesterol, 340 mg sodium

Breakfast Dishes

Finding appealing, lowfat, quick-to-fix breakfast foods can be a real challenge. To add variety to your usual fare, sample the four choices we offer here.

■ *Pictured on page 83*

Cantaloupe & Yogurt Shakes

Preparation time: About 10 minutes

> 2   medium-size cantaloupes (about 2 lbs. *each*)
> ¼   cup lime or lemon juice
> 2   cups vanilla or plain nonfat yogurt
> 2   to 3 tablespoons sugar

Cut each cantaloupe in half; scoop out and discard seeds. Then, using a spoon, scoop fruit from rinds into a blender or food processor; discard rinds. To fruit in blender, add lime juice, yogurt, and sugar. Whirl until smoothly blended. Pour into 4 tall glasses. Makes 4 servings.

Per serving: 179 calories (2% fat, 83% carbohydrates, 15% protein), 0.5 g total fat (0 g saturated fat), 39 g carbohydrates, 7 g protein, 3 mg cholesterol, 93 mg sodium

Fruit-filled Burritos

Preparation time: About 5 minutes
Microwaving time: 1 to 2 minutes

> 1   large flour tortilla (9 to 10 inches in diameter)
> 2   tablespoons part-skim ricotta cheese or light cream cheese
> ½   cup sliced strawberries or whole raspberries
> ½   to 1 teaspoon sugar

Spread tortilla with ricotta cheese; top with strawberries and sprinkle with sugar. Fold opposite sides of tortilla over filling, then roll from one end to enclose. Set tortilla, seam side down, on a microwave-safe plate; rub lightly all over with water. Microwave, uncovered, on **HIGH (100%)** until tortilla is hot to touch (1 to 2 minutes), checking after 1 minute. Makes 1 serving.

Per serving: 192 calories (14% fat, 71% carbohydrates, 15% protein), 3 g total fat (2 g saturated fat), 34 g carbohydrates, 7 g protein, 10 mg cholesterol, 248 mg sodium

Peach Shortcakes

Preparation time: About 20 minutes
Baking time: About 15 minutes

> 1   cup all-purpose flour
> 2   teaspoons baking powder
> ¼   teaspoon baking soda
> 3   tablespoons margarine
> ⅓   cup lowfat buttermilk
> 1   cup lowfat cottage cheese
> 3   tablespoons honey
> ⅛   teaspoon ground nutmeg
> 2   large firm-ripe peaches (about 1 lb. *total*)
>   Additional honey (optional)

In a medium-size bowl, stir together flour, baking powder, and baking soda until well blended. Using a pastry blender or your fingers, cut in or rub in margarine until mixture resembles coarse meal. Add buttermilk and stir just until dry ingredients are evenly moistened.

Turn dough out onto a lightly floured board and knead gently just until smooth (about 1 minute). Divide dough into fourths. Pat each portion into a 3-inch-diameter round; place rounds well apart on an ungreased baking sheet.

Bake in a 450° oven until lightly browned (about 15 minutes). Transfer to a rack and let cool slightly.

Meanwhile, whirl cottage cheese, the 3 tablespoons honey, and nutmeg in a blender or food processor until smooth. Peel, pit, and slice peaches.

To serve, split each biscuit in half horizontally. Set bottom halves on 4 plates; top each with a fourth of the cottage cheese mixture and a fourth of the peach slices. Cover lightly with biscuit tops. Serve with additional honey, if desired. Makes 4 servings.

Per serving: 326 calories (26% fat, 60% carbohydrates, 14% protein), 10 g total fat (2 g saturated fat), 49 g carbohydrates, 12 g protein, 3 mg cholesterol, 616 mg sodium

Muffins with Apple-Almond Spread

Preparation time: About 10 minutes
Cooking time: About 3 minutes

> ¼   cup chopped almonds
> ½   cup unsweetened applesauce
> ⅓   cup lowfat cottage cheese
> 1   tablespoon sugar
> ½   teaspoon ground cinnamon
> ⅛   teaspoon ground nutmeg
> 1   teaspoon grated orange peel (optional)
> 4   to 6 English muffins, split and toasted

Toast almonds in a small frying pan over medium heat until golden brown (about 3 minutes), stirring. Remove from heat and set aside. In a food processor or blender, combine applesauce, cottage cheese, sugar, cinnamon, and nutmeg. Whirl until smoothly puréed. Stir in orange peel (if desired) and almonds. Spread over hot muffin halves. Makes 4 to 6 servings.

Per serving: 200 calories (20% fat, 66% carbohydrates, 14% protein), 5 g total fat (0.5 g saturated fat), 33 g carbohydrates, 7 g protein, 1 mg cholesterol, 352 mg sodium

■ *Pictured on page 11*

Spring Dove Breads

Preparation time: About 1 hour, plus about 1½ hours for dough to rise

Baking time: 12 to 15 minutes

You're guaranteed delighted smiles all around when you serve these fanciful bird-shaped breads at a spring brunch. The recipe produces a dozen plump rolls, each large enough for two to share.

2	**cups warm water (about 110°F)**
1	**package active dry yeast**
2	**tablespoons margarine, at room temperature**
1	**tablespoon honey**
3	**cups whole wheat flour**
2	**to 2½ cups unbleached all-purpose flour**
24	**raisins or currants**
12	**whole blanched almonds**
1	**egg yolk beaten with 1 tablespoon water**

Pour water into a large bowl; sprinkle with yeast. Let stand for 5 minutes to soften yeast, then mix in margarine and honey. Stir in whole wheat flour and 2 cups of the all-purpose flour.

To knead with a dough hook, beat until dough is stretchy and cleans sides of bowl (8 to 10 minutes).

To knead by hand, stir until dough is evenly moistened, then scrape dough onto a floured board and knead until smooth and velvety (about 10 minutes), adding more all-purpose flour as needed. Place dough in an oiled bowl; turn dough over to oil top.

Cover bowl of dough (kneaded by either method) with plastic wrap. Let dough rise in a warm place until doubled (about 1 hour). Punch down dough, then knead briefly on a lightly floured board to expel air.

Divide into 12 equal portions; cover with plastic wrap to keep from drying out.

Shape doves as shown in illustrations below, working with one portion of dough at a time. Pinch off a ¾-inch ball for dove head and put back under plastic wrap. Roll remainder of dough piece into a 9-inch-long tapered rope measuring about ½ inch across at one end, about 1 inch across at the other. Loop thin end of rope to form an overhand knot. Set dough on a nonstick or greased baking sheet. For dove's tail, make 2 or 3 lengthwise cuts in wide end of rope and pull apart to resemble tail feathers. Cover with plastic wrap and refrigerate while you shape remaining dove bodies (remember to pinch a ball of dough for head off each large piece of dough). Place dove bodies at least 2 inches apart on baking sheets (you'll need 2 baking sheets).

To shape dove heads, roll each reserved ball of dough into a smooth teardrop shape. Settle heads into cavities of dough knots (poke an indentation with your finger, if needed); press down firmly to secure.

Make a small slash on each side of each head; insert raisins for eyes. Make a small slash at front of each head and insert an almond (wide end first) for beak. Cover with plastic wrap and let rise in a warm place just until puffy (about 30 minutes).

Before baking doves, push raisins and almonds back into heads to secure them. Brush doves lightly with egg yolk mixture. Bake in a 375° oven until golden (12 to 15 minutes). Serve hot; or let cool on a rack, then serve at room temperature. Makes 12 rolls (24 servings).

Per serving: 112 calories (14% fat, 73% carbohydrates, 13% protein), 2 g total fat (0.5 g saturated fat), 21 g carbohydrates, 4 g protein, 9 mg cholesterol, 13 mg sodium

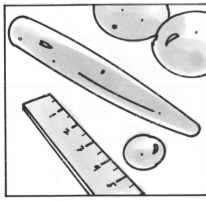  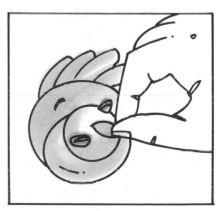

Pinch a ball from each section of dough for dove head; roll rest of dough into a tapered rope.

Knot bread rope from thin end. Slash wide end for tail; for head, insert teardrop-shaped dough in cavity.

Slash sides of head and insert raisin eyes; slash front of head and insert almond for beak.

Desserts

For diet-conscious dessert lovers, there's good news galore: you can satisfy your sweet tooth with an almost limitless variety of treats that are low in fat yet deliciously rich in flavor.

Juicy fresh fruit, usually almost entirely fat free, is a delectable choice at any time of year. Serve it unadorned—or, for something a bit more glamorous, add a simple embellishment: a touch of brown sugar, a dusting of vanilla-scented powdered sugar, or a sprinkle of freshly grated nutmeg or white chocolate. Or present assorted ripe fruits with a simple dip such as our smooth French Cream. If you're serving tropical fruits, try heating them in the oven or microwave with a little honey and a squeeze of citrus. You can also bake your favorite fruits beneath a crumbly, sweetly spiced blanket of sugar, flour, and a touch of polyunsaturated vegetable oil margarine.

When you make a cake or cookies, look for recipes containing egg whites rather than whole eggs or yolks—it's the egg yolk that carries the fat (the white has none).

Every now and then, treat yourself to lowfat and nonfat frozen desserts. Most fruit ices have no fat, and they're easy to make in your own freezer or ice cream maker. In the market, look for commercial nonfat and lowfat frozen yogurt and other frozen treats with less than two percent milk fat; luscious new flavors seem to be created almost every day.

They're flecked with crisp nuts and gilded with tart icing—but
Lemon-tipped Pistachio Biscotti (recipe on page 96) are still low in fat.
Serve the crunchy slices with fresh fruit and espresso or wine. The
traditional accompaniment for sipping is vin santo, a sweet Italian
dessert wine made from partially dried grapes.

Minted Raspberries with White Chocolate

Preparation time: About 15 minutes, plus 30 minutes to cool syrup

Chilling time: At least 2 hours

For a lovely summer dessert, embellish plump ripe raspberries with a refreshing mint syrup and a light shower of grated white chocolate.

Mint Syrup (recipe follows)

6 cups raspberries

1 ounce white chocolate, grated

Prepare Mint Syrup; let cool and chill as directed.

Shortly before serving, spoon raspberries into 4 dessert dishes; drizzle each serving with a fourth of the syrup, then sprinkle each with a fourth of the chocolate. Makes 4 servings.

■ *Mint Syrup.* In a 1-quart pan, bring ⅓ cup **water** to a boil over high heat. Stir in 6 tablespoons **sugar** and ¼ cup firmly packed chopped **fresh mint.** Boil until reduced to ⅓ cup (2 to 3 minutes). Remove from heat and let stand for 30 minutes. Pour syrup through a fine wire strainer into a jar; discard mint leaves. Cover and refrigerate for at least 2 hours or up to a month.

Per serving: 202 calories (13% fat, 83% carbohydrates, 4% protein), 3 g total fat (0 g saturated fat), 45 g carbohydrates, 2 g protein, 1 mg cholesterol, 6 mg sodium

Cherries, Berries & French Cream

Preparation time: About 10 minutes

This smooth, lightly sweetened blend of lowfat cottage cheese and sour cream is reminiscent of the French dessert cheese called *coeur à la crème*. For a pretty presentation, center the bowl of cheese on a platter or in a flat basket; then surround with whole strawberries and cherries for dipping. (You can use either dark or golden sweet cherries.)

½ cup lowfat cottage cheese

1 to 2 tablespoons light sour cream

1½ tablespoons powdered sugar

¼ teaspoon vanilla

⅛ teaspoon ground nutmeg

2 cups strawberries

2 cups sweet cherries (with stems)

In a blender or food processor, combine cottage cheese, 1 tablespoon of the sour cream, sugar, vanilla, and nutmeg. Whirl until smooth, adding more sour cream as necessary to give cheese mixture a good dipping consistency. (At this point, you may cover and refrigerate for up to a day.)

To serve, mound cheese mixture in a small bowl; arrange strawberries and cherries around it. To eat, dip fruit into cheese mixture. Makes 4 to 6 servings.

Per serving: 92 calories (12% fat, 71% carbohydrates, 17% protein), 1 g total fat (0 g saturated fat), 17 g carbohydrates, 4 g protein, 1 mg cholesterol, 98 mg sodium

Hot Papaya Sundaes

Preparation time: About 15 minutes

Baking time: About 15 minutes

In early spring, before other fresh fruits have reached the marketplace, papayas from the tropics are often abundantly available. Use the luscious golden fruits in this simple, dramatic hot-and-cold dessert.

- 1 **tablespoon margarine, melted**
- ½ **teaspoon grated lime peel**
- ⅓ **cup rum or water**
- ¼ **cup lime juice**
- 3 **tablespoons honey**
- 2 **small firm-ripe papayas (about 1 lb. *each*)**
- 2 **cups vanilla lowfat frozen yogurt**

In a 9- by 13-inch casserole, stir together margarine, lime peel, rum, lime juice, and honey. Cut unpeeled papayas in half lengthwise; scoop out and discard seeds, then place papaya halves, cut sides down, in honey mixture. Bake in a 375° oven until papayas are heated through and sauce is beginning to bubble (about 15 minutes).

Carefully transfer hot papaya halves, cut sides up, to dessert plates; let stand for about 5 minutes. Meanwhile, stir pan juices in casserole to blend; pour into a small pitcher. Fill each papaya half with small scoops of frozen yogurt; offer pan juices to pour over sundaes to taste. Makes 4 servings.

Per serving: 279 calories (15% fat, 77% carbohydrates, 8% protein), 4 g total fat (1 g saturated fat), 47 g carbohydrates, 5 g protein, 5 mg cholesterol, 96 mg sodium

Peach & Raspberry Crisp

Preparation time: About 15 minutes

Baking time: About 45 minutes

Peaches and raspberries ripen at about the same time—a fortunate coincidence for dessert lovers, who can enjoy the two fruits together in tempting treats like this one. If you like, top each sweet serving with a scoop of frozen yogurt.

- 8 **medium-size firm-ripe peaches (about 2 lbs. *total*)**
- ⅔ **cup sugar**
- 2 **tablespoons lemon juice**
- ½ **teaspoon ground cinnamon**
- 2 **cups raspberries**
- ⅔ **cup all-purpose flour**
- ¼ **teaspoon ground nutmeg**
- ¼ **cup cold margarine, diced**
  Vanilla lowfat frozen yogurt (optional)

Peel and slice peaches (you should have about 4 cups). In a shallow 1½- to 2-quart casserole, combine peaches, ⅓ cup of the sugar, lemon juice, and cinnamon; mix lightly. Spread raspberries over peach mixture.

In a food processor or a medium-size bowl, whirl or stir together flour, remaining ⅓ cup sugar, and nutmeg until well blended. Add margarine; whirl with on-off bursts (or cut in with a pastry blender or 2 knives) until mixture begins to cling together in lumps. Spoon over raspberries.

Bake in a 375° oven until fruit mixture is bubbly in center and topping is golden brown (about 45 minutes). Let cool for at least 10 minutes; serve warm or at room temperature. Top with frozen yogurt, if desired. Makes 8 servings.

Per serving: 207 calories (25% fat, 71% carbohydrates, 4% protein), 6 g total fat (1 g saturated fat), 38 g carbohydrates, 2 g protein, 0 mg cholesterol, 68 mg sodium

Soaked in an apple-rum syrup spiced with coriander seeds, Liqueur Pound Cake (recipe on facing page) is delightful with your favorite fruits—try juicy whole strawberries or raspberries, sliced nectarines or peaches, or fresh pineapple rings. Mint sprigs make a pretty garnish for the serving plate.

Liqueur Pound Cake

Preparation time: *About 30 minutes*

Baking time: *About 40 minutes*

Fine-textured and tender, this syrup-soaked loaf is almost devoid of fat—it's made with egg whites only, and contains no shortening at all.

> **Vegetable oil cooking spray**
> **Cake flour to dust pan**
> 1 **cup sifted cake flour**
> 1 **teaspoon baking soda**
> ½ **teaspoon baking powder**
> 6 **egg whites (about ¾ cup), at room temperature**
> 1¼ **cups sifted powdered sugar**
> 1 **teaspoon vanilla**
> **Apple-Liqueur Syrup (recipe follows)**

Spray a 4½- by 8½-inch loaf pan with cooking spray; dust pan with flour, then tap to remove excess. Set pan aside.

In a medium-size bowl, stir together the 1 cup flour, baking soda, and baking powder until well blended. Set aside. In large bowl of an electric mixer, beat egg whites at high speed until foamy. Gradually add sugar, beating until whites barely hold soft peaks; beat in vanilla. Add flour mixture; beat just until well mixed. Spread batter in prepared pan.

Bake in a 300° oven until top of cake is golden brown and edges are just beginning to pull away from pan (about 40 minutes). Meanwhile, prepare Apple-Liqueur Syrup.

Use a slender spatula to loosen hot cake from pan. Carefully invert pan and turn out cake onto a rack. Pour ¼ cup of the syrup into pan, then return cake to pan. Using a slender skewer, pierce cake all over at 1-inch intervals (pierce all the way through to bottom). Slowly pour 6 to 7 tablespoons more syrup over top of cake; pour remaining syrup into a small pitcher or serving bowl. Let cake cool in pan to room temperature. If made ahead, cover and refrigerate cake and syrup separately for up to 2 days; reheat syrup before serving, if desired.

To serve, invert cake onto a platter; cut into about ½-inch-thick slices. Offer remaining syrup to add to taste. Makes 16 servings.

■ *Apple-Liqueur Syrup.* In a 2-quart pan, combine 1 can (6 oz.) **frozen apple juice concentrate,** ½ cup **rum,** 2 tablespoons **amaretto,** 1 tablespoon **lemon juice,** and 1 teaspoon **coriander seeds.** Bring to a boil over high heat; boil until reduced to 1 cup (5 to 8 minutes). Use hot or cool.

Per serving: 103 calories (2% fat, 89% carbohydrates, 9% protein), .2 g total fat (0 g saturated fat), 19 g carbohydrates, 2 g protein, 0 mg cholesterol, 89 mg sodium

Amaretti-topped Fresh Pineapple Pie

Preparation time: *About 25 minutes, plus 15 minutes for filling to stand*

Baking time: *About 50 minutes*

Crushed almond macaroons stand in for a top crust in this juicy fresh fruit pie. The filling is a simple blend of pineapple chunks, sugar, and tart lime.

> **Lowfat Pastry (page 96)**
> ¼ **cup quick-cooking tapioca**
> ¾ **cup sugar**
> 5 **cups ½-inch chunks fresh pineapple**
> ½ **teaspoon grated lime peel**
> 1 **tablespoon lime juice**
> 1¼ **cups coarsely crushed almond macaroons (about 24 cookies, *each* 1¼ inches in diameter)**

Prepare Lowfat Pastry and set aside in pie pan.

In a large bowl, stir together tapioca and sugar. Add pineapple, lime peel, and lime juice; mix gently. Let stand for at least 15 minutes.

Spoon pineapple filling into pastry; place pan on a baking sheet to catch drips. Bake in a 400° oven for 30 minutes. Sprinkle crushed macaroons over pineapple filling, then continue to bake until filling is bubbly all over and pastry is golden brown (18 to 20 more minutes). Let cool slightly on a rack before cutting. Makes 8 servings.

Per serving: 310 calories (18% fat, 78% carbohydrates, 4% protein), 6 g total fat (1 g saturated fat), 63 g carbohydrates, 3 g protein, 0 mg cholesterol, 69 mg sodium

Orange Blossom Strawberry Pie

Preparation time: About 15 minutes

Cooking time: 17 to 20 minutes

Chilling time: At least 1 hour

Cutting down on shortening gives the lowfat pastry for this pie a crisper texture; adding a little sugar makes it tender. Bake the crust first, then fill it with whole ripe strawberries and an orange-accented fresh strawberry glaze.

    Lowfat Pastry (recipe follows)
 6 to 7 cups strawberries, hulled
 6 tablespoons water
 ¾ cup sugar
 2 tablespoons cornstarch
 1 teaspoon grated orange peel
 2 to 3 tablespoons orange-flavored liqueur;
    or 2 tablespoons frozen orange juice
    concentrate, thawed

Prepare Lowfat Pastry. Pierce all over with a fork to prevent puffing, then bake in a 425° oven until golden (12 to 15 minutes). Let cool in pan on a rack.

Measure 2 cups of the least perfect strawberries. Place in a blender or food processor, add water, and whirl until puréed. In a 1½-quart pan, stir together sugar, cornstarch, and orange peel. Mix in strawberry purée. Cook over medium-high heat, stirring often, until mixture comes to a full boil (about 5 minutes). Stir in liqueur.

Arrange remaining 4 to 5 cups berries, tips up, in cooled pastry shell. Evenly spoon hot cooked berry purée over whole berries to cover completely. Refrigerate, uncovered, until purée is cool and set (at least 1 hour). If made ahead, cover lightly and refrigerate for up to a day. Makes 8 servings.

■ *Lowfat Pastry.* In a medium-size bowl or a food processor, combine 1 cup **all-purpose flour** and 1½ teaspoons **sugar;** stir together or whirl until well blended. Add ¼ cup cold **margarine;** cut in with a pastry blender or 2 knives (or whirl with on-off bursts) until mixture resembles coarse crumbs. Gradually add 2 to 3 tablespoons **cold water**, mixing lightly with a fork (or whirling briefly) until mixture begins to hold together. Pat into a flat, smooth round.

On a lightly floured board, roll out pastry into a 12-inch circle. Ease pastry into a 9-inch pie pan. Trim edge, fold under, and flute decoratively.

Per serving: 241 calories (24% fat, 72% carbohydrates, 4% protein), 6 g total fat (1 g saturated fat), 43 g carbohydrates, 2 g protein, 0 mg cholesterol, 69 mg sodium

■ *Pictured on page 91*

Lemon-tipped Pistachio Biscotti

Preparation time: About 35 minutes

Baking time: 25 to 28 minutes

Here's a temptingly pretty version of the classic twice-baked Italian cookies called *biscotti;* each crisp slice is dotted with pale green pistachios and tipped with a tangy lemon glaze. Serve with frothy after-dinner espresso, or offer alongside fresh fruit or a tart sorbet or fruit ice.

 2   cups all-purpose flour
 2   teaspoons baking powder
 ¼   cup margarine, at room temperature
 ⅔   cup sugar
 1½   teaspoons grated lemon peel
 1   egg
 2   egg whites (about ¼ cup)
 1   teaspoon vanilla
 ½   cup shelled salted roasted pistachio nuts,
      coarsely chopped
      Lemon Icing (recipe on facing page)

In a medium-size bowl, stir together flour and baking powder until well blended; set aside. In a large bowl, beat together margarine, sugar, and lemon peel until well blended. Beat in egg, then egg whites. Beat in vanilla. Gradually add flour mixture, beating until well blended. Stir in pistachios.

Divide dough in half. On a lightly floured board, shape each portion into a long loaf about 1½ inches in diameter. Place loaves about 3 inches apart on a greased baking sheet; flatten each loaf to a thickness of about ½ inch. Bake in a 350° oven until firm to the touch (15 to 18 minutes).

Remove baking sheet from oven; cut hot loaves crosswise into about ½-inch-thick slices. Turn slices cut sides down and spread out slightly on baking sheets (you will need at least 2 baking sheets). Return to oven and continue to bake until biscotti look dry and are lightly browned (about 10 more minutes). Transfer biscotti to racks and let cool.

Prepare Lemon Icing; spread icing over about 1 inch of one end of each cookie. Let stand until icing is firm (about 15 minutes). Makes about 54 cookies.

■ *Lemon Icing.* In a small bowl, stir together 1 cup sifted **powdered sugar** and ½ teaspoon **grated lemon peel.** Stir in 1 to 1½ tablespoons **lemon juice,** using just enough to give icing a good spreading consistency.

Per cookie: 50 calories (28% fat, 65% carbohydrates, 7% protein), 2 g total fat (0 g saturated fat), 8 g carbohydrates, 1 g protein, 4 mg cholesterol, 34 mg sodium

Raspberry-filled Cocoa Meringues

Preparation time: About 45 minutes, plus 2 hours to dry meringues

Cooking time: About 1 hour

Piped from a pastry bag, an airy cocoa-flavored meringue makes individual cups with jauntily pointed "lids"—perfect containers for a fresh raspberry filling. Baking the fragile meringues on parchment makes it easy to remove them from the baking sheets when they're done.

> **5** **egg whites (about 10 tablespoons), at room temperature**
> ½ **teaspoon cream of tartar**
> 1¼ **cups sugar**
> ¼ **cup unsweetened cocoa**
> **Raspberry Filling (recipe follows)**
> **Unsweetened cocoa**
> **Raspberries and mint sprigs (optional)**

Cut 2 sheets of baking parchment to fit 2 baking sheets. On each sheet of parchment, trace eight 2½-inch-diameter circles, spacing circles 1 inch apart. Place parchment on baking sheets; set aside.

In large bowl of an electric mixer, beat egg whites and cream of tartar at high speed until frothy. Gradually add sugar, 1 tablespoon at a time, beating until whites hold stiff, moist peaks and sugar is dissolved. Gradually add the ¼ cup cocoa, beating until well blended; scrape bowl often.

Spoon meringue into a pastry bag fitted with a ½-inch-wide star tip. Twist top of bag to enclose meringue. To make each cup, pipe meringue onto a traced circle on one sheet of parchment, starting in center of circle and spiraling out to fill area evenly within the outline. Then pipe another meringue layer around outer edge of first layer to form a rim (cups should be about 1½ inches tall). Repeat to make 7 more cups.

To make each top, pipe meringue around edge of a circle on second sheet of parchment; then spiral in to fill area evenly. Then pipe a smaller circle atop the first, continuing the spiral to make a cone-shaped mound about 1½ inches tall.

Bake tops and cups in a 250° oven until meringues are firm to the touch (about 1 hour); switch pan positions halfway through baking. Turn off oven and let meringues dry in closed oven for 2 hours. (At this point, you may package meringues airtight and store at room temperature for up to a week.)

Prepare Raspberry Filling. To assemble desserts, place meringue cups on a platter; spoon an eighth of the filling into each, then cover with a meringue top. Dust lightly with cocoa. Garnish with raspberries and mint sprigs, if desired. Makes 8 servings.

■ *Raspberry Filling.* You will need 2 cups **raspberries**. Place 1 cup of the berries in a blender or food processor, add 2 tablespoons **water,** and whirl until puréed. In a small pan, stir together ⅓ cup **sugar** and 2 teaspoons **cornstarch;** mix in raspberry purée. Cook over medium-high heat, stirring often, until mixture comes to a full boil (2 to 3 minutes). Remove from heat; if desired, press through a strainer to remove seeds. Stir in 1 tablespoon **framboise,** kirsch, or light rum; let cool for 10 minutes. Stir in remaining 1 cup raspberries.

Per serving: 192 calories (3% fat, 91% carbohydrates, 6% protein), 1 g total fat (0 g saturated fat), 46 g carbohydrates, 3 g protein, 0 mg cholesterol, 35 mg sodium

Black Forest Cocoa Angel Food Cake

Preparation time: About 40 minutes

Cooking time: About 45 minutes

Just a little unsweetened cocoa gives this moist and lofty angel food cake its tempting chocolate flavor. Fill the cake with cherries, spread with a fluffy icing—and you've turned a simple lowfat dessert into a real dazzler.

¾	**cup sifted cake flour**
¼	**cup unsweetened cocoa**
1½	**cups powdered sugar**
12	**egg whites (about 1½ cups), at room temperature**
1½	**teaspoons cream of tartar**
⅛	**teaspoon salt**
1	**cup granulated sugar**
1½	**teaspoons vanilla**
¼	**teaspoon almond extract**
	Tart Cherry Filling (recipe follows)
	Fluffy Frosting (recipe follows)
2	**tablespoons kirsch**
	Chocolate curls (optional)

Sift flour, cocoa, and powdered sugar into a bowl; set aside. In large bowl of an electric mixer, beat egg whites, cream of tartar, and salt at high speed until foamy. Gradually add granulated sugar, about 2 tablespoons at a time, beating until mixture holds stiff peaks. Gently fold in vanilla and almond extract. Sprinkle flour-cocoa mixture, ¼ cup at a time, over meringue; using a rubber spatula, fold in gently after each addition just until flour mixture disappears. Turn batter into an ungreased 10-inch tube pan with a removable bottom; gently smooth top. Gently draw spatula through batter to eliminate large air bubbles.

Bake in a 375° oven until top of cake springs back when lightly touched (about 35 minutes). Invert pan on a funnel to keep cake from shrinking; let cool completely.

Meanwhile, prepare Tart Cherry Filling. Just before assembling dessert, prepare Fluffy Frosting.

Remove cake from pan. Using a serrated knife, cut cake horizontally into 3 layers. Sprinkle bottom layer with 1 tablespoon of the kirsch; spread with a very thin layer of Fluffy Frosting, then with half the Tart Cherry Filling. Add middle layer. Sprinkle with remaining 1 tablespoon kirsch; spread thinly with frosting, then spread with remaining filling. Cover with top layer; spread sides and top of cake with remaining frosting. If made ahead, let stand, uncovered, at room temperature for up to 6 hours. Decorate with chocolate curls before serving, if desired. Makes 12 servings.

■ *Tart Cherry Filling.* Drain 1 can (about 1 lb.) **pitted tart red cherries,** reserving liquid. Measure ½ cup of the liquid and set aside; discard remaining liquid. In a small pan, mix ½ cup **sugar** and 2 tablespoons **cornstarch.** Stir in cherries and the ½ cup **reserved cherry liquid.** Bring to a boil over medium heat, stirring; boil, stirring constantly, until thickened and clear. Then boil for 1 more minute. Remove from heat and stir in 1 tablespoon **kirsch.** Let cool.

■ *Fluffy Frosting.* In top of a double boiler, combine 2 **egg whites** (about ¼ cup), at room temperature; ½ cup **light corn syrup;** ½ cup **sugar;** and a pinch of **salt.** Beat with an electric mixer at high speed until blended. Place over rapidly boiling water and cook, beating constantly, until frosting holds stiff peaks (about 4 minutes). Remove from heat and beat for 1 more minute. Beat in ½ teaspoon **vanilla** and 1 or 2 drops **red food coloring,** if desired. Use while warm.

Per serving: 318 calories (1% fat, 93% carbohydrates, 6% protein), .4 g total fat (0 g saturated fat), 74 g carbohydrates, 5 g protein, 0 mg cholesterol, 121 mg sodium

Frozen Italian Chocolate Tartufi

Preparation time: About 10 minutes, plus 1 hour to cool pudding

Cooking time: About 20 minutes

Freezing time: At least 5 hours

Scoops of silky-textured frozen pudding, rolled in ground semisweet chocolate and dusted with snowy powdered sugar, make an irresistible dessert.

- ½ **cup unsweetened cocoa**
- 1 **tablespoon cornstarch**
- 1 **cup granulated sugar**
- 1 **cup nonfat milk**
- ½ **cup water**
- 3 **egg whites (about 6 tablespoons), at room temperature**
- ½ **cup semisweet chocolate chips**
  Powdered sugar

In a 1- to 1½-quart pan, stir together cocoa, cornstarch, and ½ cup of the granulated sugar until well blended. Whisk in milk. Cook over medium heat, stirring, until pudding boils and thickens (about 10 minutes). Remove from heat. Place a sheet of plastic wrap directly atop pudding so it touches surface of pudding. Let stand at room temperature until cool (about 1 hour); do not refrigerate.

When pudding is almost cool, combine water and remaining ½ cup granulated sugar in a 1- to 1½-quart pan; bring to a boil over high heat. Boil without stirring until a candy thermometer registers 260°F (8 to 12 minutes).

About 2 minutes before sugar syrup is ready, place egg whites in large bowl of an electric mixer; beat at high speed until whites hold stiff peaks. With mixer running, pour in sugar syrup in a slow stream (take care to avoid pouring syrup onto moving beaters); continue to beat at high speed until mixture holds stiff peaks.

Using a rubber spatula, gently fold cooled pudding into egg white mixture until well blended. Transfer to an 8-inch-square pan, cover, and freeze until firm (at least 4 hours) or for up to a day.

Place chocolate chips in a food processor or blender; whirl until finely ground, then pour onto a piece of wax paper. Scoop frozen pudding into 6 equal portions. Using 2 large spoons or your hands, quickly roll each portion into a rough ball. Roll in ground chocolate to coat. Place balls slightly apart in a chilled shallow pan. Freeze until firm (at least 1 hour) or for up to 2 weeks; cover if stored for more than a few hours.

To serve, place each ball in a chilled dessert dish, then sprinkle lightly with powdered sugar. Makes 6 servings.

Per serving: 250 calories (18% fat, 74% carbohydrates, 8% protein), 5 g total fat (1 g saturated fat), 49 g carbohydrates, 5 g protein, 1 mg cholesterol, 49 mg sodium

Ginger-Peach Ice

Preparation time: About 30 minutes, plus 1 hour to chill

Freezing time: At least 2 hours

Just five ingredients go into this ginger-tingled champagne ice. It's a cooling treat you can easily make in your freezer (or use a self-refrigerated ice cream machine, following the manufacturer's directions).

- 1½ **cups water**
- ½ **cup sugar**
- 2 **tablespoons minced crystallized ginger**
- 1 **cup champagne or sparkling apple juice**
- 3 **tablespoons peach-flavored liqueur**
  Mint sprigs (optional)

In a 1- to 2-quart pan, combine water, sugar, and 1 tablespoon of the ginger; bring to a boil over high heat, stirring. Remove from heat and let cool, then stir in champagne and liqueur. Cover and refrigerate until cold (about 1 hour).

Pour mixture into a shallow 2- to 3-quart metal pan; cover and freeze until solid (at least 2 hours) or for up to a month. Then, using a heavy spoon, break mixture into chunks. Whirl in a food processor or beat with an electric mixer to form a smooth slush. (For a firmer texture, return slushy ice to freezer for up to 1 hour.)

To serve, spoon ice into chilled dessert glasses. Sprinkle with remaining 1 tablespoon ginger; garnish with mint sprigs, if desired. Makes 6 to 8 servings.

Per serving: 111 calories (0% fat, 100% carbohydrates, 0% protein), 0 g total fat (0 g saturated fat), 20 g carbohydrates, 0 g protein, 0 mg cholesterol, 5 mg sodium

Appendix

For help in designing your lowfat eating plan, consult the useful guides and references in this chapter. We begin with a glossary of terms commonly used by nutritionists; look here if you're unsure of the difference between saturated and unsaturated fat or don't know just what fiber is. Next, to assist you in planning menus and in cutting down on fat in cooking, we offer a chart detailing the four food groups, a table of lower-fat substitutions for some common recipe ingredients, and a discussion of lowfat cooking techniques. We also provide recipes for unsalted chicken broth and a fluffy whipped topping that's almost fat-free. And to help you shop wisely, we explain how to read package labels to evaluate a food's fat content.

Finally, we include a chart of healthy weight limits for a range of ages and heights (see page 105) and four pages of tables offering nutritional information for a number of common foods.

Glossary

Atherosclerosis. Process in which the lining of the arteries becomes coated with fatty substances. Blood vessels are narrowed and scarred by the deposits and may eventually become completely blocked. If the blockage occurs in an artery supplying blood to the heart, a heart attack results; if it occurs in an artery supplying blood to the brain, a stroke results.

Calorie. Measurement of the amount of energy produced when food is metabolized.

Carbohydrates. One of the three major nutrients supplying energy to the body (the other two are fat and protein). Providing fiber and about 4 calories per gram, carbohydrates are our most efficient source of energy, more readily available for use by the body than either protein or fat. They are essential for proper function of the brain and nervous system.

Carbohydrates are categorized as simple or complex. *Simple carbohydrates* are found in honey, syrups, jams, jellies, fruit, and fruit juices. *Complex carbohydrates*, classified as water soluble or water insoluble, are found in most fruits and vegetables and in foods such as whole grains, breads, and legumes.

Cholesterol. A waxy, fatlike substance essential to the structure of cell membranes and nerve sheaths and the production of vitamins and hormones. The liver manufactures sufficient cholesterol for the body's needs; dietary cholesterol comes from the foods we eat. Cholesterol is present in all foods of animal origin: meats, poultry, fish, eggs, and dairy products.

Both dietary cholesterol and the cholesterol synthesized in the body affect the amount of cholesterol circulating in the bloodstream. This amount, measured in milligrams per deciliter, is known as the *blood cholesterol level*.

Dietary fiber. The undigested portion of food. Found only in plants, dietary fiber is either soluble or insoluble. Some types of fiber may help lower blood cholesterol. (For more on fiber, see page 5.)

Fats. One of the three major nutrients supplying energy to the body (the other two are carbohydrates and protein). Providing about 9 calories per gram, fats play an important role in cell maintenance and vitamin absorption.

Fats are classified as saturated or unsaturated; unsaturated fats are further categorized as monounsaturated or polyunsaturated. *Saturated fats*, usually solid at room temperature, are typically found in foods of animal origin (such as meat and whole-milk dairy products) and in some vegetable products (palm and coconut oils, for example). Saturated fats tend to raise blood cholesterol.

Unsaturated fats, generally liquid at room temperature, most often come from plants and may help lower blood cholesterol. *Monounsaturated fats* include olive, peanut, and avocado oils; among *polyunsaturated fats* are corn, safflower, and sesame oils.

Hydrogenated fats such as margarine and vegetable shortening are polyunsaturated oils that have been converted to a more saturated form through the addition of hydrogen (a commercial process called hydrogenation). These fats tend to increase blood cholesterol.

Omega-3 fatty acids, a group of polyunsaturated fats found primarily in coldwater marine fish such as salmon and tuna, may help lower cholesterol levels.

Lipoproteins. Fat-protein molecules that carry cholesterol in the blood. *High-density lipoprotein* (HDL), known as "good cholesterol," may be responsible for carrying cholesterol away from cells and tissues back to the liver for elimination. It's assumed to protect against atherosclerosis. *Low-density lipoprotein* (LDL), often termed "bad cholesterol," may be responsible for depositing cholesterol on the artery walls. A higher LDL level is assumed to indicate a greater risk of atherosclerosis.

Protein. One of the three major nutrients supplying energy to the body (the other two are fat and carbohydrates). Protein provides about 4 calories per gram; it's made up of amino acids, substances essential to maintaining healthy muscles, bone, skin, and blood. Animal products provide *complete protein*, protein that contains all eight of the amino acids required for good health. Plant products (except soybeans) provide *incomplete protein*, supplying less than the full range of essential amino acids. You can usually correct such deficiencies by combining plant foods (by mixing grains with legumes, for example).

Triglycerides. The major component of fatty tissues, triglycerimdes are blood fats manufactured by the liver from excess dietary fats, carbohydrates, and alcohol. No direct relationship has been determined between levels of triglycerides and the risk of heart disease, but individuals with very high triglyceride counts may be advised to lose weight (if they are overweight) and to limit or avoid alcohol and concentrated sugars.

The Four Food Groups

Nutritionists have assigned each of the basic food groups a recommended number of servings per day, based on the needs of normal adults. Children, teenagers, and pregnant and nursing women have specific dietary needs that should be addressed by a dietitian or physician. Fats are not included here; for information on how much fat to eat each day, see "How fats & cholesterol affect your health" (page 5).

MILK & MILK PRODUCTS*

2 servings per day

Milk (1 cup)

Cheese, hard (1¼ oz.)

Cottage cheese (2 cups)

Yogurt, plain (1 cup)

Buttermilk (1 cup)

*To cut back on fat intake, choose lowfat or nonfat varieties when possible.

MEAT & MEAT ALTERNATIVES

2 servings per day

Meat, lean (2 to 3 oz., cooked weight)

Poultry (2 to 3 oz., cooked weight)

Fish (2 to 3 oz., cooked weight)

Eggs (2)*

Cheese, hard (2 oz.)

Cottage cheese (½ cup)

Dried peas or beans (1 cup cooked)

Peanut butter (¼ cup)

Nuts and seeds (½ cup)

Tofu (1 cup)

*The American Heart Association recommends limiting your intake to 4 eggs per week.

FRUITS & VEGETABLES*

4 servings per day

Apple, banana, orange, pear, tomato
(1 medium-size)

Grapefruit (½ medium-size)

Melon (½ medium-size)

Russet or thin-skinned potato, sweet potato
(1 medium-size)

Vegetables, cut up (½ cup)

Fruits, cut up (½ cup)

Salad greens (1 cup)

Vegetable/fruit juices (½ cup)

*Category includes fresh, frozen, and canned.

GRAINS, BREADS & CEREALS*

4 servings per day

Bread (1 slice)

Bagel (½ of 3-inch-diameter bagel)

Cooked cereal (½ to ¾ cup)

Dry cereal (1 oz.)

Pasta (½ to ¾ cup cooked)

Rice (½ to ¾ cup cooked)

Pita bread (½ of 6-inch-diameter bread)

Dinner roll (1 oz.)

Tortilla (about 7-inch diameter)

*To obtain adequate fiber, choose whole-grain varieties when possible.

Substitutions for Reducing Fat & Cholesterol

Instead of	Choose
Bacon	Canadian bacon
Beef, regular ground	Extra-lean ground beef or ground skinned turkey breast (or half of each)
Butter	Polyunsaturated margarine with liquid oil listed as the first ingredient
Buttermilk	For each cup, use 1 tablespoon lemon juice or distilled white vinegar plus enough nonfat milk to equal 1 cup; or use nonfat or lowfat buttermilk.
Cheese	Lowfat cheeses such as part-skim mozzarella and part-skim ricotta. Use nonfat or lowfat cottage cheese; use Romano or Parmesan in small quantities.
Chicken, whole	Skinned chicken breast
Chocolate, unsweetened	For each ounce, use 3 tablespoons unsweetened cocoa plus 1 tablespoon salad oil.
Cream	Evaporated skim milk
Cream, whipped	Lowfat Whipped Topping (page 105)
Eggs	For every 2 whole eggs, use 1 egg plus 2 egg whites.
French-fried potatoes	Garlic Potatoes (page 76)
Ice cream	Frozen nonfat or lowfat yogurt, fruit ices, and sherbets
Mayonnaise	Light mayonnaise or half mayonnaise and half plain nonfat yogurt
Milk, whole	Nonfat milk
Peanuts	Pretzels
Potato chips	Air-popped popcorn (spray with vegetable oil cooking spray so seasonings such as chili powder or cinnamon will adhere)
Salad dressings	Lowfat bottled dressings or homemade dressings (such as those on page 36)
Shortening, solid	Unsaturated vegetable oil
Sour cream	Plain nonfat or lowfat yogurt or light sour cream
Tuna or sardines packed in oil	Tuna or sardines packed in water

Light Ways to Cook Old Favorites

Once you've mastered a few fat-cutting cooking techniques, you'll be able to prepare your favorite dishes without using as much butter, margarine, or oil as the standard recipes specify. And if you prefer to avoid not only excess fat but also wine and other alcoholic beverages in cooking, you'll want to consult our suggestions for nonalcoholic substitutions.

To help you cook the lowfat way, we've included two recipes in this section. The first is a flavorful unsalted chicken broth, the second a surprisingly simple whipped topping that adds a frothy finishing touch to lowfat desserts.

■ *Braise-deglaze.* Recipes for soups, stews, and sauces often begin with chopped vegetables (such as onions, garlic, leeks, carrots, celery, and bell peppers) cooked in butter or oil to develop a flavor base. You can also achieve rich flavor using fat-free liquids—and little or no actual fat. For example, if a recipe calls for 3 to 4 tablespoons fat, omit it altogether. Instead, put the vegetables in the specified cooking pan, then almost cover them with a liquid that will complement the flavor of the finished dish—broth, dry wine, or just plain water. To promote some sizzle, you may add a small amount of unsaturated fat; as little as 1 teaspoon is sufficient.

Boil over high or medium-high heat, uncovered, stirring occasionally, until the liquid cooks away and the vegetables begin to brown and stick to the pan. Then add more liquid, 2 tablespoons at a time, stirring to release the browned bits from the pan (the vegetables will absorb the brown color). Repeat this reduction and deglazing process until the color is rich and appealing; watch closely to prevent scorching. Once the vegetables are as browned as you like, simply proceed as the recipe directs.

Chicken Vermicelli Carbonara (page 49) uses the braising-deglazing technique.

■ *Oven braise-deglaze.* You can braise and deglaze in the oven as well as on top of the range. Follow the directions above, but use a shallow rimmed baking pan in a 450° oven; start with ¼ cup liquid, then pour in additional liquid in ¼-cup portions. The initial reduction will take about 15 minutes. Use a wide spatula to stir in subsequent amounts of liquid.

■ *Oven-fry.* Small pieces of food (such as meatballs, cut-up chicken or meat, or sliced vegetables), arranged in a single layer and lightly coated with vegetable oil or olive oil cooking spray, brown well in a hot oven (400° to 500°, depending on the food). Be sure to leave enough space between the pieces to let moisture evaporate quickly. Simply Perfect Eggplant (page 79) uses this technique.

■ *Use more egg whites* and fewer whole eggs or egg yolks. Egg whites serve much the same function as whole eggs in many recipes, and omitting all or most of the yolks reduces fat, calories, and cholesterol.

■ *Fill in with water.* For cutting calories, nothing beats using water instead of fat. Fat gives sauces and dressings a smooth, rich feel in the mouth, but you can achieve a similar velvety quality without using much fat; just replace some or all of it with slightly thickened water or other liquid (as appropriate to the dish).

Popular thickeners include all-purpose flour, cornstarch, arrowroot, and potato starch. Flour can withstand the most heat without breaking down, but it makes an opaque sauce and requires several minutes of simmering to eliminate any starchy flavor. Cornstarch produces a clearer mixture that tastes cooked as soon as it comes to a boil; arrowroot and potato starch also make very clear sauces that lose any starchy taste just before reaching a boil. (In supermarkets, arrowroot is usually found with the spices, potato starch with the flours or specialty foods.)

For each cup of liquid, use 1 tablespoon flour for a thin sauce, 2 tablespoons for a medium sauce, and 3 to 4 tablespoons for a thick sauce. If you're using cornstarch, arrowroot, or potato starch, you need just half these amounts of starch to produce the same thickening effect.

To streamline sauces that combine flour or another starch with melted fat or oil, omit the fat or oil; dilute the starch with some of the liquid used in the sauce, then cook as directed. Shallot Dressing (page 36) and Hunter's-style Lamb Stew (page 44) illustrate this technique.

■ *Nonalcoholic alternatives.* If you prefer not to cook with alcoholic ingredients such as wine, you can still prepare most of the dishes in this book with delicious results. If a recipe is made with a substantial amount (¼ cup or more) of dry red or white wine or sherry, simply increase the other liquid called for (usually water, broth, or fruit or tomato juice) by that amount. When you taste the food for seasoning, you may want to compensate for the omission of wine by adding a few drops of lemon juice.

Sweet dessert wines such as port or Madeira can be replaced by fruit juices such as orange, apple, grape, or cranberry; make sure the color of the juice is appropriate to the finished dish.

In place of almond, anise, or mint liqueurs, you can use a few drops of the corresponding extract (though these are also alcohol-based) mixed with enough water to make up the amount of liquid specified. Instead of orange and other fruit-flavored liqueurs, use an undiluted fruit juice concentrate.

Homemade Chicken Broth

Preparation time: About 30 minutes, plus 4 hours to chill
Cooking time: About 3 hours

- 5 **pounds bony chicken pieces (wings, backs, necks, carcasses)**
- 2 **large onions, cut into chunks**
- 2 **large carrots (about 8 oz. *total*), cut into chunks**
- 6 **to 8 parsley sprigs**
- ½ **teaspoon whole black peppercorns**
- 3½ **quarts water**

Rinse chicken pieces and place in a 6- to 8-quart pan. Add onions, carrots, parsley sprigs, peppercorns, and water. Bring to a boil over high heat; reduce heat, cover, and simmer for 3 hours. Let cool.

Pour broth through a fine strainer into a bowl; discard chicken and vegetable scraps. Cover broth and refrigerate for at least 4 hours or up to 2 days. Lift off and discard fat. To store, freeze in 1- to 4-cup portions. Makes about 10 cups.

Per cup: *Due to variations in ingredients and cooking time, precise nutritional data is not available. The nutritional value of this broth is roughly similar to that of canned low-sodium chicken broth.*

Lowfat Whipped Topping

Chilling time: At least 1 hour
Preparation time: About 5 minutes

- ½ **cup evaporated skim milk**
- 1 **tablespoon powdered sugar**
- ¼ **teaspoon vanilla**

Pour milk into bowl of an electric mixer. Cover bowl; then refrigerate milk and beaters for 1 hour. Beat milk at high speed until fluffy (30 seconds to 1 minute). Add sugar and vanilla; continue to beat until mixture holds soft peaks. Serve immediately. Makes 6 to 8 servings.

Per serving: *19 calories (0% fat, 70% carbohydrates, 30% protein), 0 g total fat (0 g saturated fat), 3 g carbohydrates, 1 g protein, 1 mg cholesterol, 21 mg sodium*

What is a healthy weight for you?

The guidelines below will help you judge if your weight is within the range suggested for persons of your age and height. Note that the table shows higher weights for people 35 years and above than for younger adults; recent research indicates that gaining a little extra weight with age does not significantly increase health risks.

Suggested Weights for Adults

Height (without shoes)	Weight in pounds* (without clothes) 19 to 34 years	35 years and over	Height (without shoes)	Weight in pounds* (without clothes) 19 to 34 years	35 years and over
5'0"	97–128	108–138	5'10"	132–174	146–188
5'1"	101–132	111–143	5'11"	136–179	151–194
5'2"	104–137	115–148	6'0"	140–184	155–199
5'3"	107–141	119–152	6'1"	144–189	159–205
5'4"	111–146	122–157	6'2"	148–195	164–210
5'5"	114–150	126–162	6'3"	152–200	168–216
5'6"	118–155	130–167	6'4"	156–205	173–222
5'7"	121–160	134–172	6'5"	160–211	177–228
5'8"	125–164	138–178	6'6"	164–216	182–234
5'9"	129–169	142–183			

* The higher weights in the ranges generally apply to men, who tend to have more muscle and bone; the lower weights more often apply to women, who have less muscle and bone.
Source: Dietary Guidelines for Americans, Third Edition, 1990
U.S. Department of Agriculture, U.S. Department of Health and Human Services

How to Read Food Labels

No cholesterol! No fat! These claims are made for many foods. How do you verify and interpret such statements? When you buy any canned or packaged food, it pays to understand nutrition labels—especially when it comes to calculating the percentage of calories provided by fat.

Nutrition information must be provided for any food to which nutrients have been added or for which health claims are made. The information is given in a standard form. The serving size and servings per container are listed, followed by the calorie, protein, carbohydrate, and fat content per serving. Amounts of sodium, cholesterol, and saturated and unsaturated fat may or may not be listed. Next, the label shows the percentage of the U.S. Recommended Daily Allowances for protein, vitamins, and minerals provided by one serving. Finally, the ingredients are listed in descending order by weight.

■ **Determining the calorie breakdown.** Look at the following sample label information, similar to that you might find on a snack food package.

> *Nutrition Information Per Serving:*
> *Serving size: 1 oz.*
> *Servings per container: 4*
> *Calories: 160*
> *Protein (grams): 3*
> *Carbohydrates (grams): 12*
> *Fat (grams): 11*
> *Sodium (milligrams): 10*
> *Cholesterol (milligrams): 0*

To calculate the percentage of calories from fat in any food, multiply the number of grams of fat per serving by 9. In our example, 11 x 9 = 99. Divide the fat calories by the total calories: 99 ÷ 160 = 0.62. Then multiply this figure by 100 to find the percent: 0.62 x 100 = 62%. Keep in mind that the American Heart Association (AHA) recommends that no more than 30% of your daily calories come from fat.

The AHA also recommends that about 55% of the day's calories come from carbohydrates. To determine carbohydrate calories, multiply the grams of carbohydrates per serving by 4; in our example, 12 x 4 = 48. Then follow the procedure just outlined for fat: divide your answer by the total calories and multiply by 100 to get the percentage. Thus, 48 ÷ 160 = 0.30; 0.30 x 100 = 30%. You can use the same method to determine the percent of protein calories, because protein, like carbohydrates, provides about 4 calories per gram.

What you've learned from our sample label, then, is that the product, though cholesterol-free, contains about 62% fat and 30% carbohydrates—just about the reverse of the situation you'd like to see for daily calorie intake. You'd be better off choosing a snack that is not only low in cholesterol, but also lower in fat and higher in carbohydrates.

NOTE: The 4-9-4 formula—4 calories per gram of protein, 9 calories per gram of fat, and 4 calories per gram of carbohydrates—is a very useful approximation, but it is not exact. A detailed nutritional analysis must also account for other factors: non-nutritive fiber in some carbohydrates, for example, and calories from alcohol (which occurs naturally in some fresh fruits). For this reason, when you check our data with the 4-9-4 formula, the numbers may not always agree precisely.

■ **Using the ingredient list.** You can read the ingredient list to confirm claims made about a food. For instance, if no ingredients from animal sources are listed, the food can be accurately described as cholesterol-free. However, it may still be high in saturated fats, which tend to raise blood cholesterol.

You can also use the list in other ways. To limit your intake of saturated fat, for example, choose a margarine that lists partially hydrogenated oil after liquid oil; that way you'll be getting more unsaturated fat than saturated (remember that the label lists ingredients in descending order by weight).

Be aware that manufacturers are permitted to list fats with the explanation "contains one or more of the following." If you're trying to avoid saturated fat, you may decide not to purchase a product that includes in its list of ingredients a statement such as "contains one or more of the following: soybean and/or palm kernel oil." Such information doesn't tell you whether the food contains saturated, unsaturated, or both kinds of fat.

Food Tables

Food/Portion	Calories	Total Fat (grams)	Saturated Fat (grams)	Protein (grams)	Carbohydrates (grams)	Cholesterol (milligrams)
POULTRY, SEAFOOD & MEATS						
Poultry						
Chicken breast, meat and skin, roasted (3½ oz.)	195	8	2	30	0	83
Chicken breast, meat only, roasted (3½ oz.)	164	4	1	31	0	84
Chicken thigh, meat and skin, roasted (3½ oz.)	245	15	4	25	0	92
Chicken thigh, meat only, roasted (3½ oz.)	207	11	3	26	0	94
Chicken liver, simmered (3½ oz.)	156	5	2	24	0	626
Turkey, light meat, meat and skin, roasted (3½ oz.)	197	8	2	29	0	76
Turkey, light meat, meat only, roasted (3½ oz.)	153	3	1	30	0	68
Turkey, dark meat, meat and skin, roasted (3½ oz.)	221	12	3	27	0	89
Turkey, dark meat, meat only, roasted (3½ oz.)	184	7	2	28	0	87
Turkey giblets (gizzard, heart, liver), simmered (3½ oz.)	166	5	2	26	0	415
Turkey, ground, cooked (3½ oz.)	227	14	4	24	0	68
Turkey, ground, skinned breast meat, cooked (3½ oz.)	153	3	1	30	0	68
Duck, meat and skin, roasted (3½ oz.)	334	28	10	19	0	83
Duck, meat only, roasted (3½ oz.)	189	7	2	29	0	88
Finfish						
Cod, Atlantic, cooked, dry heat (3½ oz.)	104	*	*	23	0	55
Flounder, cooked, dry heat (3½ oz.)	116	2	*	24	0	67
Halibut, cooked, dry heat (3½ oz.)	139	3	*	26	0	41
Mackerel, cooked, dry heat (3½ oz.)	260	18	4	24	0	74
Redfish, cooked, dry heat (3½ oz.)	120	2	*	24	0	55
Salmon, sockeye, grilled (3½ oz.)	216	11	2	27	0	87
Sea bass, cooked, dry heat (3½ oz.)	123	3	*	23	0	53
Snapper, cooked, dry heat (3½ oz.)	127	2	*	26	0	47
Swordfish, cooked, dry heat (3½ oz.)	154	5	1	25	0	50
Trout, rainbow, cooked, dry heat (3½ oz.)	150	4	*	26	0	72
Tuna, white, canned in oil, drained (3½ oz.)	185	8	n/a	26	0	31
Tuna, white, canned in water, drained (3½ oz.)	135	2	*	26	0	42
Shellfish						
Clams, cooked, moist heat (3½ oz.)	147	2	*	25	0	66
Crab, Alaskan king, cooked, moist heat (3½ oz.)	96	2	*	19	0	53
Lobster, cooked, moist heat (3½ oz.)	97	*	*	20	0	71
Oysters, raw (3½ oz.)	68	2	*	7	0	55
Scallops, raw (3½ oz.)	87	*	*	17	0	33
Shrimp, cooked, moist heat (3½ oz.)	98	1	*	21	0	193
Beef						
Flank steak, lean only, broiled (3½ oz.)	205	10	4	27	0	66
Porterhouse, broiled (3½ oz.)	303	22	9	25	0	82
Prime rib, cooked (3½ oz.)	355	29	12	22	0	83
Round steak, lean only, broiled (3½ oz.)	190	7	3	29	0	77
Tenderloin, lean only, broiled (3½ oz.)	209	10	4	28	0	83
Ground, extra-lean, broiled (3½ oz.)	254	16	6	25	0	83
Ground, lean, broiled (3½ oz.)	270	18	7	25	0	86
Ground, regular, broiled (3½ oz.)	287	21	8	24	0	89
Liver, braised (3½ oz.)	160	5	2	24	0	386
Veal						
Ground, cooked (3½ oz.)	171	8	3	24	0	102
Loin chop, lean only, braised (3½ oz.)	224	9	3	33	0	124

* Contains less than 1 gram

Food/Portion	Calories	Total Fat (grams)	Saturated Fat (grams)	Protein (grams)	Carbohydrates (grams)	Cholesterol (milligrams)
Lamb						
Leg, shank portion, lean only, roasted (3½ oz.)	179	7	2	28	0	86
Loin chops, lean only, broiled (3½ oz.)	214	10	3	30	0	94
Rack rib, roasted (3½ oz.)	356	30	13	21	0	96
Pork						
Bacon, pan-fried (3½ oz.)	572	49	17	30	0	84
Canadian bacon, grilled (3½ oz.)	184	8	3	24	0	58
Fresh ham, lean only (3½ oz.)	219	11	4	29	0	95
Center loin, broiled (3½ oz.)	314	22	8	27	0	96
Shoulder, roasted (3½ oz.)	323	25	9	22	0	95
Tenderloin, roasted (3½ oz.)	165	5	2	29	0	92
Ham, boneless, canned, roasted (3½ oz.)	226	15	5	21	0	62
Spareribs, braised (3½ oz.)	394	30	12	29	0	120
FRUIT						
Apple (1 med.)	81	*	*	*	21	0
Apricots, dried (8 halves)	67	*	*	1	17	0
Avocado (1 med.)	324	31	5	4	15	0
Banana (1 med.)	105	*	*	1	27	0
Cantaloupe (½ cup)	28	*	*	*	7	0
Cherries, sweet (10 large)	49	*	*	*	11	0
Dates, dried (2)	46	*	*	*	12	0
Grapefruit (½ grapefruit)	38	*	*	*	10	0
Grapes, seedless (½ cup)	57	*	*	*	14	0
Orange, peeled (1 med.)	69	*	*	1	17	0
Peach (1 med.)	56	*	*	*	15	0
Pear (1 med.)	98	*	*	*	25	0
Pineapple, fresh (½ cup)	38	*	*	*	10	0
Plum (1 med.)	36	*	*	*	9	0
Prunes, dried (3)	60	*	*	*	16	0
Raisins (2 tbsp.)	54	*	*	*	14	0
Raspberries (½ cup)	30	*	*	*	7	0
Strawberries (½ cup)	23	*	*	*	5	0
Watermelon (½ cup)	26	*	*	*	6	0
VEGETABLES						
Artichokes, globe, cooked (1 med.)	53	*	*	3	12	0
Asparagus, fresh, cooked (½ cup)	23	*	*	2	4	0
Beans, green, fresh, cooked (½ cup)	22	*	*	1	5	0
Beans, lima, large dry, cooked (½ cup)	108	*	*	7	20	0
Broccoli, fresh, cooked (½ cup)	23	*	*	2	4	0
Cabbage, green, raw, shredded (½ cup)	8	*	*	*	2	0
Carrots, fresh, raw (½ cup)	24	*	*	*	6	0
Corn, fresh, cooked (½ cup)	89	1	*	3	21	0
Lettuce, green leaf (½ cup)	5	*	*	*	*	0
Mushrooms, fresh, raw (½ cup)	9	*	*	*	2	0
Peas, green, frozen, cooked (½ cup)	62	*	*	4	11	0
Pepper, bell, chopped (½ cup)	13	*	*	*	3	0
Potato, baked with skin (1 med.)	220	*	*	5	51	0
Potato, boiled, peeled (½ cup)	67	*	*	1	16	0
Potato, sweet, baked in skin, peeled (1 med.)	117	*	*	2	28	0
Spinach, fresh, raw (½ cup)	6	*	*	*	*	0
Squash, summer, fresh, cooked (½ cup)	18	*	*	*	4	0
Squash, winter, fresh, cooked (½ cup)	40	*	*	*	9	0
Tomatoes, fresh (½ cup)	17	*	*	*	4	0

* Contains less than 1 gram

Food/Portion	Calories	Total Fat (grams)	Saturated Fat (grams)	Monounsaturated Fat (grams)	Polyunsaturated Fat (grams)	Cholesterol (milligrams)
OILS						
Canola (rapeseed) (1 tbsp.)	120	14	*	8	4	0
Coconut (1 tbsp.)	120	14	12	*	*	0
Corn (1 tbsp.)	120	14	2	3	8	0
Cottonseed (1 tbsp.)	120	14	4	2	7	0
Grapeseed (1 tbsp.)	120	14	1	2	10	0
Olive (1 tbsp.)	120	14	2	10	1	0
Palm (1 tbsp.)	120	14	7	5	1	0
Palm kernel (1 tbsp.)	120	14	11	2	*	0
Peanut (1 tbsp.)	120	14	2	6	4	0
Safflower (1 tbsp.)	120	14	1	2	10	0
Sesame (1 tbsp.)	120	14	2	5	6	0
Soybean (1 tbsp.)	120	14	2	6	5	0
Sunflower (1 tbsp.)	120	14	1	3	9	0
Walnut (1 tbsp.)	120	14	1	3	9	0

Food/Portion	Calories	Total Fat (grams)	Saturated Fat (grams)	Protein (grams)	Carbohydrates (grams)	Cholesterol (milligrams)
BREADS, PASTA, GRAINS, LEGUMES, NUTS						
Bread, rye (1 oz.)	69	*	*	3	15	*
Bread, white, enriched (1 oz.)	57	*	*	2	14	*
Bread, whole wheat (1 oz.)	69	1	*	3	13	*
Crackers, graham (4 squares)	109	3	*	2	21	0
Crackers, saltine (10)	123	3	*	3	20	0
Doughnut, raised, glazed (1)	170	10	2	2	19	11
English muffin (1)	130	1	*	4	26	n/a
Roll, frankfurter or hamburger (1)	119	2	*	3	21	2
Roll, hard (1)	156	2	*	5	30	2
Tortilla, corn (1)	67	1	*	2	3	0
Macaroni, cooked (½ cup)	99	*	*	3	20	0
Noodles, egg, cooked (½ cup)	106	1	*	4	20	26
Rice, brown, cooked (½ cup)	108	*	*	3	22	0
Rice, white, enriched, cooked (½ cup)	132	*	*	3	29	0
Beans, black, dried, cooked (½ cup)	114	*	*	8	20	0
Beans, pinto, dried, cooked (½ cup)	117	*	*	7	22	0
Lentils, dried, cooked (½ cup)	115	*	*	9	20	0
Soybeans, dried, cooked (½ cup)	149	8	1	14	9	0
Almonds, whole, shelled (1 oz.)	167	15	1	6	6	0
Cashews, salted, roasted in oil (1 oz.)	163	14	3	5	8	0
Peanuts, salted, roasted in oil (1 oz.)	165	14	2	7	5	0
Peanut butter (1 tbsp.)	95	8	1	5	3	0
Pecans, halves (1 oz.)	189	19	2	2	5	0
Walnuts, English, pieces (1 oz.)	182	18	2	4	5	0
OTHER FATS, EGGS, DAIRY						
Butter (1 tbsp.)	102	12	7	*	*	31
Lard (1 tbsp.)	116	13	5	*	*	12
Margarine, corn oil, hard (stick) (1 tbsp.)	102	11	2	*	*	0
Margarine, safflower, soft (tub) (1 tbsp.)	101	11	1	0	0	0
Mayonnaise, whole-egg (1 tbsp.)	99	11	2	*	*	8
Vegetable shortening, hydrogenated (1 tbsp.)	113	13	3	0	0	0
Egg, whole, raw (1 large)	75	5	2	6	*	213

* Contains less than 1 gram

Food/Portion	Calories	Total Fat (grams)	Saturated Fat (grams)	Protein (grams)	Carbohydrates (grams)	Cholesterol (milligrams)
OTHER FATS, EGGS, DAIRY ((continued))						
Egg yolk, raw (1)	59	5	2	3	*	213
Egg white, raw (1)	17	0	0	4	*	0
Buttermilk, cultured (1 cup)	98	2	1	8	12	10
Condensed milk, sweetened, canned (¼ cup)	246	7	4	6	42	26
Evaporated milk, skim, canned (¼ cup)	50	*	*	5	7	3
Evaporated milk, whole, canned (¼ cup)	84	5	3	4	6	18
Milk, whole (1 cup)	149	8	5	8	11	34
Milk, lowfat, 2% (1 cup)	122	5	3	8	12	20
Milk, skim or nonfat (1 cup)	86	*	*	8	12	5
Milk, whole, chocolate (1 cup)	208	8	5	8	26	30
Creamer, nondairy, liquid (1 tbsp.)	20	2	*	*	2	0
Creamer, nondairy, powder (2 tbsp.)	64	4	4	*	6	0
Half-and-half (1 tbsp.)	20	2	1	*	*	6
Sour cream (1 tbsp.)	31	3	2	*	*	6
Sour cream, light (1 tbsp.)	25	2	1	1	1	5
Whipping cream (1 tbsp.)	43	5	3	*	*	17
Whipped cream, pressurized (1 tbsp.)	10	*	*	*	*	3
Dessert topping, nondairy (1 tbsp.)	9	*	*	*	*	*
Yogurt, whole, plain (8 oz.)	138	7	5	8	11	29
Yogurt, lowfat, plain (8 oz.)	143	4	2	12	16	14
Yogurt, lowfat, fruit-flavored (8 oz.)	231	2	2	10	43	9
Yogurt, nonfat, plain (8 oz.)	127	*	*	13	17	5
Cheese						
American (1 oz.)	106	9	6	6	*	27
Blue (1 oz.)	100	8	5	6	*	21
Brie (1 oz.)	95	8	n/a	6	*	28
Cheddar (1 oz.)	114	9	6	7	*	30
Cheese spread, process, American (1 oz.)	87	6	4	5	2	16
Cottage cheese, creamed (½ cup)	108	5	3	13	3	16
Cottage cheese, dry curd (½ cup)	62	*	*	13	1	5
Cottage cheese, lowfat, 2% fat (½ cup)	102	2	1	16	4	9
Cream cheese (1 oz.)	99	10	6	2	*	31
Gouda (1 oz.)	101	8	5	7	*	32
Gruyère (1 oz.)	117	9	5	8	*	31
Jack (1 oz.)	106	9	n/a	7	*	25
Mozzarella, whole milk (1 oz.)	80	6	4	6	*	22
Mozzarella, part skim (1 oz.)	72	5	3	7	*	16
Neufchâtel (1 oz.)	74	7	4	3	*	22
Parmesan (1 oz.)	129	9	5	12	1	22
Ricotta, whole milk (½ cup)	214	16	10	14	4	63
Ricotta, part skim (½ cup)	170	10	6	14	6	38
Roquefort (1 oz.)	105	9	5	6	*	26
Swiss (1 oz.)	107	8	5	8	*	26
Frozen Desserts						
Frozen yogurt, lowfat (½ cup)	113	1	n/a	3	23	4
Frozen yogurt, nonfat (½ cup)	110	0	0	2	24	0
Ice cream, rich, 16% fat (½ cup)	175	12	7	2	16	44
Ice cream, regular, 10% fat (½ cup)	134	7	4	2	16	30
Ice milk, regular (½ cup)	92	3	2	3	14	9
Ice milk, soft serve (½ cup)	112	2	1	4	19	7
Sherbet, orange (½ cup)	135	2	1	1	39	7

* Contains less than 1 gram

Index